Also by Boom

*101 Things Every Woman Should Know About Men*

For more information about Big Boom or his books, visit:

www.bigboombooks.com

www.bodyguardforwomenshearts.com

# IF YOU WANT CLOSURE
# IN YOUR RELATIONSHIP,
# START WITH YOUR LEGS

## ~ A Guide to Understanding Men ~

## BIG BOOM

A FIRESIDE BOOK
PUBLISHED BY SIMON & SCHUSTER
NEW YORK   LONDON   TORONTO   SYDNEY

FIRESIDE
Rockefeller Center
1230 Avenue of the Americas
New York, NY 10020

Copyright © 2007 by Big Boom Freeman

First Fireside Edition 2007

FIRESIDE and colophon are registered trademarks
of Simon & Schuster, Inc.

For information regarding special discounts for bulk purchases,
please contact Simon & Schuster Special Sales at 1-800-456-6798
or business@simonandschuster.com.

Designed by Susan Yang

Manufactured in the United States of America

10   9   8   7   6   5   4   3

Library of Congress Cataloging-in-Publication Data

Boom, Big.
    If you want closure in your relationship, start with your legs : a guide to
    understanding men / by Big Boom.
        p. cm.
    1. Man-woman relationships.   2. Interpersonal relations.   3. African
American women—Psychology.   4. African American men—Psychology.
    5. Love.   6. Sex.   I. Title.

HQ801.B753 2007
306.73089'96073—dc22                                                    2006100666
ISBN-13: 978-1-4165-4646-7
ISBN-10:    1-4165-4646-4

This book is dedicated with love and affection to:
My grandmother, Earlene Berry, my secret angel who
had faith in me long before it was reasonable.
Oh God how blessed I am! I have traveled a mighty
long journey. For this I am grateful! I am also
grateful for the angels in my life, seen and unseen.
They guide, protect, and support me.

# DEAR READER,

Boom and I share a great friendship and marriage. The struggle between two strong minds sometimes brought friction in our relationship, but little did we dream where we'd be today.

I look at him now and remember where he came from. Boom has changed drastically, learned to control the power of his thoughts and words, and freed himself from his past.

His mission is to help women find strength through adversity. He has become a God fearing man who has fully dedicated his life to God's vision. Boom is the Bodyguard of my heart. His voice, his touch, even a quick glance in my direction, always sends shivers throughout my soul. I could not be more proud to have him as my husband.

Boom's enthusiasm for life, his family and me is truly inspiring. I am blessed to have him in my life. I can trust and depend on his protection and his honesty—even when I may not want to hear it. He's strengthened my own faith and ability to hope, believe and dream.

We have put God first and this has made our friendship and marriage stronger and our home happier. We have come to know the true treasure of a great relationship. I hope that by reading this book you, too, will be on your way to knowing your worth and the relationship you deserve.

Sincerely,
Lauren Freeman

# ACKNOWLEDGMENTS

I am grateful for the people whose paths cross mine and lives make mine richer, more joyful, and more successful. I am especially thankful to the following people for their hand in opening doors along my path that enable me to grow and to share divinely inspired wisdom with those who open up and listen. Thank you to:

My wife Lauren, the spirit of my life. Thank you for being lovingly supportive of my work and listening patiently as I ponder new ideas and thoughtfully sharing ideas of your own. I love you.

To my mother Shirley Freeman, for giving me life; without you none of this would have been possible. To my family and friends for your love, support, and undying enthusiasm. I recognize that not everyone is blessed with a family and friends as loving or so true. I love you.

Bishop T.D. Jakes, my spiritual advisor, for the inspiring example you set and whose sermon brought forth the birth to this book.

Larry Barnes, my strength in life for supporting me in the good and bad times, rich and poor times, and for never letting me down.

Steve Harvey, my life-long friend and employer, for showing me how to do more with my life's work in God's way.

Minister Louis Farrakahn for helping me get it in perspective and finding the missing key to life.

Denella Ri'chard, my friend and interpreter, for your support and constructive input.

Most importantly, I thank God for using me as a vessel to deliver words of inspiration, truth, and personal transformation.

# A NOTE FROM BOOM

When I first started working on *If You Want Closure in Your Relationship, Start with Your Legs,* I thought long and hard about what it would mean to women and how they could use this book to improve their lives and their relationships.

There are several important factors associated with the purpose behind this book. First, it will help expedite a woman's learning. Second, it will facilitate her journey toward personal and spiritual fulfillment. Third, it will help women avoid the common relationship pitfalls they encounter. Hopefully, this book will help women develop a more rewarding and renewed relationship.

I learned life lessons from the streets and because of those lessons, I am able to speak openly and honestly in a language that women can understand. I was one of those men who I am now advising women to stay away from. I suggest you stay away from them until God brings them in and cleans them up. I'm not telling you what I heard; I'm telling you what I know. I am the messenger! Please don't crucify the messenger: just listen to the message and learn from it.

As you read the book, it might be like finding out your preacher cheated on his wife, and now you're angry. Now you feel like the world doesn't mean anything to you. But deep down inside you know that God still speaks through this preacher.

I ask the same for me as I would ask for the cheating preacher: "Don't be so angry at us for being human that you miss the message."

I'm Boom the bodyguard for women's hearts. Women now have a protector who will guide them in the right direction and help them along their journey. You can trust and depend on me to tell you the truth. Now, let's get started!

I'm sure you have missed blessings before. But that's behind you. Don't miss the blessings in front of you.

# CONTENTS

# WHY I WROTE THIS BOOK

*I know there's a lot of no-good men out there because I used to be one.*

For the first time in my life, I understand the pain so many women have experienced because they thought men loved them. After all, I once helped cause some of that pain. I decided to write this book for several reasons. First, I promised God that if He would help me find a good woman to point me in the right direction, I would tell somebody.

Second, I feel that every woman should stop and smell the roses and enjoy what God put together for her.

The third reason, which I think is the most important reason, is that I'm not scared anymore.

## I HAD A TALK WITH GOD
As I had a heart-to-heart talk with God, I learned that if I faced fear it would disappear.

I said, "God, I'm kind of scared to do this because I think women might look down on me and embarrass me."

And He said, "She reaps what she sows." Then He said, "You weren't scared when you were looking down on women and bashing them."

All I could do was hold my head down and pray some more. Then God said, "If you do it for Me I'll make sure the women listen to you."

The old folks use to say, "You'll understand it better by and by." Now I know what they meant because right after I talked to God, something went through my spirit. I couldn't quite explain it then, but now I understand my mission. I'm bringing my message to women by way of this book.

## WAKE UP AND LISTEN

This book is not for the so-called nice girls who have never done anything wrong in their lives. The ones who have only had one man, or the ones who don't want to do anything with their lives.

If the title of this book shocked you a little, that's all right; sometimes people need to be shocked to wake up and listen.

## YOU'VE GOT TO STOP AND SMELL THE ROSES

Because God has prepared each of us to fulfill our life's destiny, it's our duty to figure out what that destiny is. When we stop our hectic schedules long enough to enjoy life, love, and happiness, we are taking the God-given opportunity to smell the roses.

## I'M NOT SCARED ANYMORE

Even though I'm no longer scared, I was a little nervous about this project. This is the first time I've written a book and it has made me think and rethink many things that have occurred in my own life. I'm ready to help women. I'm not scared of what people think, because I'm helping women become better.

## WHAT REALLY MAKES THIS BOOK
## DIFFERENT FROM OTHERS?

People often ask me, "What is this book going to be about that no one else has already written?" I tell them, "This is not a book on prostitution, but it does discuss women selling their bodies. This is not a book about battered women, but it does discuss how in the past, if a woman didn't shut her mouth she would get pimp-slapped."

This is not a book about God, but it does discuss God. You see, this kind of book has never been written before. It's raw, honest, and it's about you.

## WHAT WOMEN WILL GAIN FROM THIS BOOK

My goal here is to provide women with different solutions to their relationship issues. From this book women are reading the sweat off my back, the wrinkles in my forehead from anger and thinking all the time; they're reading that a man like me has finally grown up; a man who thought he was a man, but wasn't; a man who once had a heart harder than a rock. I was a man whose spirit was tougher than steel, and colder than ice. My blood would boil like water and my temperature would rise so high that the unthinkable would enter my mind.

No matter what you think of me, as you read this book I want you to remember that the most important thing I'm sending is a message of care and concern to women of all walks of life.

I have come a long way, from being a tough guy to finally growing up into a God-fearing, one-wife-loving, committed man. If I can get women to understand my message, then everything that I have done to get to this place was worth it.

When you're finished reading about the man I was, you will be more knowledgeable about the man I am, and you will learn a valuable lesson about how to improve your relationships and how to find closure in your unhealthy ones.

## DON'T CONDEMN ME

I'm not big on words, but I'm big in heart and big on helping women who are trying to do right in their lives. I used to be big on the tear-down of women; now I'm big on the buildup. I'm under new construction too and I want brothers to join me.

As I present you with the numerous topics in this book, my goal is to paint a picture that you can see and hear. I'm telling you the same things that your preacher is telling you—the truth. I wrote this book in my own voice, so everything is not intended to be grammatically correct; there was a picture I wanted to paint.

I want you to actually visualize and interpret what I'm saying and do your best to learn from this book. I also want you to try your best *not* to condemn me for writing this book.

## WHAT'S DIFFERENT FROM THE PREACHER'S SPEECH?

The only difference in what I'm saying and what the preacher is saying is that the preacher tells a woman what to do and she thinks she has to change her ways and do all of this or all of that—before it works. What I'm telling her is going to make her feel strong enough to go home tonight and do many of the things she needs to do to get her life back.

The preacher is telling her what God said and I'm telling her what will happen if she doesn't do what God said. A woman should think about how these remedies can help her and why there's help on both sides. If she listens to what the preacher says and gets started by using the advice he gives, she might come out of her turmoil sooner. By the time she realizes what I've said, it just might be too late for her because she messed around and waited too long before she took the proper action.

Okay, some women say, "It's never too late." Well, that's wrong because sometimes it is. Many of the things I'm discussing in this book will make the difference between whether a woman waits too late to get started or begins right on time. Evidently, what the preacher is telling women is not sinking in because they're not listening. I've put it in a street way for people who are street smart, living the club life, have been out partying a lot and been in all kinds of drama relationships.

The tips in this book will help women get things done before it's too late. Nice girls who go to church—I'm proud of you, glad for you, but don't criticize me for putting this book out for ladies who need help. Just stick with me and you'll learn some things too.

With this information women will see the error in their ways. They will learn how to make positive changes that help them move forward instead of backwards—and that's what separates this book from other books.

If you've found a man
and there's still doubt,
take a look at his life,
from the inside out!

Love Always.

IF YOU WANT CLOSURE
IN YOUR RELATIONSHIP,
START WITH YOUR LEGS

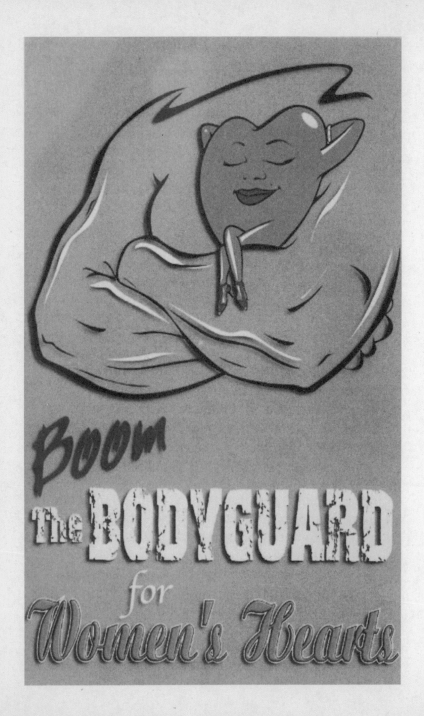

# One

# BOOM'S PERSONAL MESSAGE

*When a man moves too fast and has multiple, meaningless partners, he's only bursting blood cells and allowing bad energy to enter the woman.*

I've had good women, bad women, and sometimes I've had both at the same time. In my past, I searched for women who were whores.

I looked for women who sold their bodies and gave men their money, their food stamps, and their welfare checks. I even dated women who strip-danced. Throughout all of this I've found that opposites attract, but a whore who acts right and also has your back, she's hard to find.

I've gone as far as to make women have sex with other women and do what I want them to do, just to make me happy. I've had women who would do stupid stuff just because I asked them to do it and they wanted me around.

For about forty-seven years of my life, I was attracted to these kinds of women . . . whorish women . . . women I could have fun with. I would put women together and watch them go at it. To me it was fun having them do wild and crazy things. Now, I'm attracted to women with qualities that are totally opposite to those kinds of women.

I dated a young lady in the cocaine world for a few years, so I've seen and done it all. During this time all I did was spend money. Women would make the money and I would spend it. I was a very uncontrollable guy during that time of my life.

Through the years, when I was about forty-seven years old . . . No! . . . I'll say at the age of forty-five, I started wanting to change, but I didn't know how to change, and when I began making changes my friends would say, "We're losing you . . . we're losing another soldier, we're losing another man, we're losing another good one." This would cause me to jump back on their side and that caused me to get back into the game. I was in the game a long time and many things that it brought to my life I'll discuss in this book.

## A WOMAN'S TRUE COLORS SHINES THROUGH

I attracted lots of women because I was considered the main attraction to them. I understood the game and what the game was all about, but when I started telling women what I wanted them to do and what I wanted out of life, they would try to be that special person, but that person wasn't really who they were.

I called it my blue light special because it was like going into a discount store—the blue light directs you to the aisles where the deals are. Not knowing this, I set myself up for a fall. These same women would start tricking me and turned out to be the kind of women I didn't want. I later found out that many of the women I encountered pretended to be who they thought I wanted them to be.

Each time I entered into a new relationship and tried to make it work, the woman's true colors eventually came out and that would set me back. It made me realize that I needed to stop telling women what I wanted, because they might not be themselves but instead try to be the special of the moment in hopes of the big purchase.

As I got older I became tired of being the type of man I had become, so I decided that each year I would try to change something about myself. I would improve the areas of my life that I thought were flawed. For me, the game had run its course, it wasn't fun anymore. So I began to work on me.

## Why I Think Relationships Are Important

A woman can have a good man, but the problem could be that she's no good for that man! A man wants sex, but a woman wants romance and material possessions. Sometimes it seems as if a man and a woman are from different worlds. It's as if men are from the East Side and women are from the West Side.

In their relationships men and women may not realize how different they really are, but it's through understanding and acceptance of the obvious and less obvious differences that they can achieve a truly great relationship.

## I Was a Smooth Operator

I ran into a friend I grew up with named Stanley. He reminded me of how nervous I would get when I first started talking to girls on the phone. I was a good talker, but I would freeze up and become insecure, especially when I saw them in person.

Stanley was good at talking to the girls. He enjoyed them and had fun and they loved him. A lot of times I'd put Stanley on the phone to talk to girls. I would tell him what to say and what to ask and he didn't have a problem doing it. I learned how to do it over time and as I got older I couldn't quit talking to women.

By the time I was seventeen, I was singing in a band. They called me the ghetto kid and I had my game down.

We wrote a couple of records and some of the lyrics were:

*You played at the game and loved and lost and now the time has come for you to pay the cost. The price was high but you knew all along you'd have to pay if you did me wrong. And another part was my love was there every night and day, can't figure out why you treat me this way. I gave you joy in return for hurt, never again because it just won't work. You think I'm gone be a fool for you? You'd better hold your breath until you turn blue. You better get it together, get a brand-new start or you gone be left with a broken heart. It says . . . Quit jaw jacking, booty smacking; skinning and grinning; let's stop the chatter, let's get down to the matter.*

I will never forget it. Those were my lines. I was real smooth.

## MY REAL TURNAROUND

My real turnaround came when I married a lady I hardly even knew. I knew her from talking to her on the telephone. I thought I could take any woman, treat her real good, give her what she wanted, and I could make her be the ideal woman for me.

But that wasn't necessarily true. You see, the biggest mistake a man makes is when he believes he can make a woman do and be who he wants by giving her gifts and material things.

Since what I used to do didn't work, I asked God to help me determine what I could do for Him since nothing detrimental happened to me when I was being deceptive and doing wrong in my life. The Holy Spirit revealed to me that God saved me for this journey I am now embarking on.

Since I'm a bodyguard for the stars by trade, I decided to protect the ones (women) I've been hurting. So now people can just call me *Boom, the Bodyguard for Women's Hearts*.

Because I've changed my life, I don't have to look behind my back or turn off the cell phone before I go into my home. I want brothers to understand that I sleep peacefully now. The more women I help, the more good women will be available to provide men with what they truly need.

Women have taught me that you don't have to fight a woman in order to gain her love or dedication.

# TWO

# I'VE MADE MISTAKES

*I sincerely apologize to any woman I have hurt in the past.*

I went back to visit some of the women I hurt, because I have ruined some ladies' lives. I started making a change by apologizing to as many of them as I could find. After talking to them and explaining my side of the issue they said that they forgave me. Each of them told me the same thing: "I still love you . . . and you taught me a lesson, but I will never let another man treat me the way you did."

Looking back, I realized that none of the women I dated were really angry with me; they were hurt.

## WOMEN HAVE TAUGHT ME MANY LESSONS

I put some pain on some women. Yes, I put some pain on their hearts. I would get mad, go off and fight women because at a young age I saw my dad do it. I saw it work, so what else did I have to do? That was what I knew.

Women have taught me that you don't have to fight in order to gain their love or dedication. It's foolish for a man to put his hands on a woman in harmful ways.

I apologize to any woman I hurt in the past and I want you to know that God is working on me and working with me.

## I GREW UP UNSUPERVISED

Even though I have older brothers and sisters, I grew up unsupervised. My mother tried to take care of five kids by herself; she would leave me at home with my sisters and brothers.

After my little sister was born, the attention was no longer on me and I felt rejected. As I grew older the empty spot felt bigger. It gave birth to the feeling of insecurity in my life. I would start fights with my siblings and they would lock me out of the house. They didn't care where I went, just as long as I got off their nerves, so I hung out in the streets where I got attention. I was in the streets eight or nine hours a day until my mother got home.

I could find plenty to do in the streets and there was nobody to control me. They would try to make me sit down and learn my lesson from school. I just couldn't tune in because there was so much stuff on my mind.

## GROWING UP DYSLEXIC

I'm dyslexic, which means I read backwards. Because of this, learning was once difficult for me. Although I knew something was wrong, I didn't do anything about it. I have gone through my whole life and never read a book. I've never even read the Bible, but I know human behavior and I know right from wrong. Knowing these things has placed stories in my heart. I find myself looking at life differently because of my dyslexia. I look at life backwards. In other words, I look at people from the inside out. Throughout my life this kind of thinking has made me who I am.

## WHEN DID THE CYCLE START?

The manipulation period started back when I was going to school, when the education department failed me, or did I fail it? No one knew where my mind was. I couldn't even find myself. No one paid attention to me because I was so angry all the time and I was doing things to lash out at everybody. Many times, they threw their hands up in the air and just gave up on me.

The only time I received help was when women picked me up. They made me feel like somebody cared about me, so I got into the world of playing women so deeply that it became my whole focus.

## I FEEL GOOD ABOUT ME NOW

When I discovered that there are people sleeping on the streets, begging for dimes with college degrees, it made me feel stronger and more confident, because you can make it if you really want to.

A great man told me that I have untapped potential. In areas where I was weak God has made me strong. I pulled from that spiritual strength to survive in this world. I was weak when it came to my education, but I was strong in my street sense. I learned to use my gift of common sense to achieve the things I desired. I learned that you could make it against all odds.

## I DON'T KNOW EVERYTHING

I don't know everything about the Bible, but when I go to church I tune in and that puts messages in my head and my heart. God works with me because God takes care of babies and fools and I guess during those times I fit into the fool category.

Sometimes I don't know the perfect way to treat a woman right—or what others would say is right, because everyone's right is different. In my world it used to always be about me, but when I got married I decided it would be all about my wife. I do all the stuff for my wife that I never did for other women and I figure that ought to be pretty close to right.

Since I've done bad things to women, I'm putting it in reverse and doing the opposite of what I used to do, and so far things are going well and my wife is pretty happy.

Knowing women, I know things could change at any time, but I believe I got the hang of it for now and I'm giving it my all.

## I'VE FINALLY GOT THE HANG OF THIS THANG

For all the people who knew me from the old days and are looking down on me for not hanging in there and getting what I needed in school: I got what I needed from the streets.

I put survival over school, but I'm doing the right things now and feeling pretty good about it. I know God has blessed me.

## GOD HAS MY BACK

I'm not against education, but as I said, there are so many people with college degrees who are lying on the ground and pushing shopping carts that I feel the way I survived helped me to avoid that kind of life.

You can read this book and judge me because that's your choice. But I'm also looking at myself and seeing how far I've come and I'm trying to determine if this is the way God wants me to do it, if this is my journey.

One of the most shocking moments in my life was when I realized God had my back and I didn't have His. I decided to put it in reverse and do everything I could do just to work for God. It made me realize that I had some more work to do.

Ever since I changed my thought pattern, things have been going a lot smoother for me. I know God is looking at me, so I have to do it right, stay on the right track. As long as God has got my back—I've finally got the hang of this thang.

Just like a drug dealer, when a man is doing wrong, he won't be able to get a good night's sleep.

# Three

# KEEP YOUR LEGS CLOSED

*I was never a pimp in my heart, but I had pimpish ways.*

If a woman is caught in a bad relationship and really wants out of it, she should become dedicated to avoiding sex with the person she is trying to gain closure with. Having sex with the closing partner will only add fuel to the fire and the flame will continue. Sex not only opens her legs, it opens emotional doors for a woman, and both should remain closed to allow that flame to die.

Sex is as important to women as it is to men, but women don't let on until they've had a few sexual acts with the man. After a woman has been with the man a few times, she starts prioritizing sex just the same as the man does, but for different reasons. We're all aware that sex tends to be more important to men while for women sex is more of an act of romance, more than a pure physical act. Of course there are always exceptions!

Without a deeper understanding of this fundamental difference, women commonly underestimate the importance of a man's sexual habits and many times judge him as superficial for wanting that one thing.

If the woman admits the truth to herself she'll confess that she wants it just as bad as the man. Men don't know the right time to have sex. Because for men anytime is the right time; however, a woman does know when the time is right. But because she's more emotional, her judgment can weaken. If she stays in control, she'll discover which men only want a woman if her legs are open and she's easy. Sometimes, however, the most effective way to jump-start a relationship is to first learn what not to do.

Great relationships are God's gift to those who are committed to creating loving, supportive, positive bonds. Great sex is a woman's reward, and she deserves it as long as it is pure, wholesome, and fair. On the other hand, sex should not be used as a weapon to keep a man. Women should remember that sex can get a man, but sex cannot keep a man!

When sex gets better, suddenly the whole relationship seems to get better.

# Four

# ASK QUESTIONS

*If a woman keeps her legs closed and her mind open when she meets a man she could find out more about him.*

A woman fails to ask a man the necessary questions in the beginning. She thinks he's a great catch and doesn't want to rub him the wrong way by asking too many questions. She'll say to herself that there's plenty of time for questions later. Problem is these questions tend to come up during arguments, or after she's become frustrated with him. She'll find out that neither the man nor the relationship is what she really thought it was.

By asking essential questions up-front a woman could avoid making many dumb relationship mistakes. If she had kept her legs closed and found out who the man really was, she probably would have never messed with him in the first place and she could have saved herself a lot of heartache and embarrassment.

## FIND OUT MORE ABOUT THE MAN

If a woman keeps her legs closed and her mind open when she meets a man, she can find out more about him and if he deserves her. She can find out about his ways, his goals in life, what he likes and dislikes, and how to have a mutually enjoyable relationship.

In the beginning, when he calls she shouldn't be so quick to return his calls: she should run little tests on him and wait a while to see how he reacts when she doesn't return his call. This helps her get to know him, especially during emotional times.

## GET MORE THAN ONE PHONE NUMBER

A woman needs at least four phone numbers from a man before she starts dating him.

1. Home number
2. Work number
3. Cell number
4. Mama, best friend, uncle, sister somewhere else where he won't be the one to answer the phone.

Phone numbers are useful to a woman only if the man is available at the numbers he gave her. If a man is willing to give a woman his numbers, then at least she will know whether he is serious about spending time with her. Having his phone numbers also proves he might be telling the truth about who he is. Only then should she think about pursuing a relationship with him.

Ask a man, "What are you here for?" "What do you want with me?" If you find out that he's not trying to be specific with you, let him go about his business without you. He's not serious about a relationship with you. You can save yourself some heartache down the road.

If the woman likes the man who meets her basic qualifications, she should know the answers to the following questions before taking things further.

1. Where does he work?
2. Is he married or has been?
3. Does he have children or baby mama drama?
4. Is he currently dating anyone?
5. Is he gay or into the down-low lifestyle?
6. What are his short- and long-term goals?
7. What is his relationship with his mama like?

She shouldn't ask about his last relationship because he'll probably lie about it, or not be ready to reveal past relationships at all.

## DON'T GET EXCITED TOO SOON OVER WHAT A MAN DOES

A woman should not get excited when a man does something special that she likes early in the dating stage. She should not assume that everything is so perfect nor feel that she has to give him sex because he does nice things for her. A real man likes doing things for a woman, period. When a woman gives in to him in the early stages, she tries to make him her man by sexually pleasing him and being available at his beck and call. Then she starts anxiously waiting by the phone for his calls and many times she waits and waits and waits and no calls come in; then she's disappointed

If a woman gives in to a man too soon—sexually—his desire diminishes because he already knows what she's like in bed. He often considers her easy prey. Because the man is a hunter by nature, he'll appreciate the woman more if he has to catch her and she's not so easy to get.

If a woman doesn't jump in bed as soon as she meets a man, she'll be able to see things about him that she likes and dislikes. If she doesn't move to the bedroom too soon, she can enjoy the man. And as she begins to understand the whole man, she'll enjoy his sex more. Of course it's better to wait until you're married, then you know that he's your man.

What makes sex a form of lovemaking is the way a woman feels about the man she's with. Great lovemaking is between the ears—it's in the mind, how both the man and the woman feel about each other. She can learn the foundation of the relationship, whether the man cares for her or if he simply wants sex. She needs to know, not assume, what the relationship is about and what his expectations are before she gets too deep into the relationship with him and has parted her legs.

## WOMEN WHO TELL HALF THE TRUTH

Women want to know everything about a man. They'll ask:

- "What about you?" or "Tell me about your past relationships."
- "How were you raised and what kind of job do you have?"
- "Do you owe anybody any money?"
- "Have you ever been to jail?"
- "Are you a homosexual?"

What turns a man off is the woman always wants to know everything about him, but she only tells half the stuff he needs to know about her. For example:

1. She doesn't tell him about those lil' bad kids she has at the house who he has to help send to college.
2. She didn't tell them about the relatives she has who are always begging for something.

3. She didn't tell him that he would have to co-sign for her family members to get cars, etc.
4. She didn't tell him that her mama's rent isn't paid and he has to help pay it, so mama won't move in with them.
5. She didn't tell him any of that!

Honesty is a two-way street. A woman has to share information if she's going to learn anything about the man. But, the bigger question is . . . should she tell him all of this in the beginning or should she just wait and let him find it out on his own? She doesn't tell him, because she knows that as soon as he finds out about her baggage he's out of there and he's not looking back! Women, you have to determine if honesty is best.

God didn't give everyone everything, but He did give everyone something.

# Five

# GAMES PEOPLE PLAY

*The game is meant to be sold, not told.*

Given the way some women have mistreated men, women shouldn't get upset about the way some men feel about them. Men place women in categories according to how the woman carries herself.

There are women who pull tricks on men for a few dollars. If the man has money and material things, some women will go out of their way, will compromise their values to get with that man. It's wrong for women to do this to themselves, but they are doing it, and the brothers are playing bait-and-switch with women's bodies and emotions. Here are a few games my partners and me used to play on women back in the day.

## THE SPIDERWEB

The spiderweb is a way to a woman's heart in all the wrong ways. A man using the spiderweb is sweet to a woman for three or four months. During this time he's patient. He laughs all the time when he's with her. He does all the things she likes to do and he makes sure there are no problems in the relationship; everything is smooth.

Around the fourth month or so . . . all of a sudden he finds some kind of problem. That's how a man traps a woman because she thought he was so nice, so perfect for her. He'll get angry and make the woman think she did something wrong, so she begs him to not be angry. The woman starts trying to make things better by saying things like "Baby, I'm sorry," and "Whatever I did to you, I'm sorry."

The man never tells the woman what she's done wrong; he simply remains angry with her. The woman starts asking questions like "Baby, why are you still angry? What did I do?" The man makes the woman worry like crazy for a few days, then he tells her what she's *not* doing for him. He makes her feel bad and guilty about whatever it is she didn't do. A woman just doesn't know that she's being put in a spiderweb.

That's how a man suckers a woman into making him her priority. The woman starts buying him gifts and doing anything that he wants her to do. It doesn't matter what he wants her to do—she does it. It could go as far as making love to another woman or doing something illegal. She feels losing him is worse. She wants him to be happy.

While using the web a man will have the woman go into a store and steal just so the woman can prove to the man that she'll do anything for him. It doesn't matter what she steals just as long as the man has his way. Every woman should be careful of the spiderweb.

## THE RABBIT TRAP

For this game, imagine placing a carrot under the opening of a box that's in front of a rabbit. Dangling the carrot makes the rabbit go after it. The rabbit wants the carrot so bad that it will risk being trapped in the box just to get it.

The same scenario works on women when men dangle gifts and promises of the perfect relationship. She reaches for it, not knowing it's a trap. She has now stepped into level one of a trap with many levels. Now she's curious and wants to venture out a little more. She's headed for level two, which is worse than level one. Many more gifts await her—sweet things that pull her into the man's trap even further. Once the man has dangled enough, it won't be long until he drops the box. Now she's trapped, he thinks he owns her and he made her, and she owes him. He'll expect you to be underneath him.

## THE BIRD'S NEST
Some women are like a bird's nest that's lying on the ground. A man doesn't even have to "climb the tree" to get the bird; he simply walks over and picks up the eggs.

No work, no effort, no challenges involved. It's just that simple. The bird's nest is *easy to get,* no challenge of any kind involved. It's also just as easy to get rid of when he's done enjoying you.

## THE BUSINESS CARD HANDLER
Be careful not to get twisted by the business card handler. He's the man who's always handing his business card out. It has all this writing on it; he's trying to convince a woman that he's a successful entrepreneur.

There are plenty of these guys out there faking it, but the woman gets all excited because he has a powerful title. The woman later finds out that he's full of games.

## THE REVERSE TECHNIQUE

Here's a trick a man will use when he has cheated and is about to break a woman's heart. He knows she will find out because somebody is going to tell her, so he'll go to her first.

He'll say, "We need to talk!" While he prepares himself he'll let her ask questions. "Why did you do this or that?" "Why did you mess around on me?" He'll say, "You know what, baby, I did mess around on you and you don't have to sit here and go through any more pain and suffering . . . I'm just going to go and you can have everything. I'm not good enough for you. I don't deserve you, so I'm going to get out of your way, and you can have yourself a good life without me." He'll start packing his bags and head for the door. Now, she doesn't want to be left alone because she thinks he's going to the other woman. See, he just reversed it. She wants to get on him about why he cheated, but he has shut all that down by saying he's leaving. She doesn't even have to put him out.

She starts grabbing his legs and begging him, "Please don't leave." She yells, "We can talk about this. We can work it out."

He says to her, "No, I'm not going to stay because I'm not going to sit up for the rest of my life listening to you say things like, 'If only you hadn't messed with that lady.' "

He doesn't want to hear it anymore, so he makes her promise she won't talk about it. He then unpacks his suitcase, puts the clothes back where they belong; they get to have a great makeup session and everything is back on track. The thing is, he was already prepared to go. He even had somewhere to go just in case it didn't work out the way he planned. He always has a Plan B.

## THE PIMP GAME

There was a guy I used to run around with. We liked to play a game where we would try to bring new girls in to sell their bodies. This was a strange game. We'd take turns at it. Here's how it went down.

Say I found a new girl: I would give my friend one hundred and fifty dollars and then tell *my* girl I got a date for her. I would take her and put her in a room and let my friend mess around with her and then he would give her the hundred and fifty. That's just to break her in and see what she's going to do the first time she has a date. I had to make sure she's ready to keep going out there and selling her body. This was also to make sure she didn't undercut herself, and to take the nervousness out so she could sell her body and keep bringing me that money. Not every man is looking for a woman to pimp, but many men will test a woman to see what type of price tag she comes with.

## THE SMOKY CLOTH TECHNIQUE

Watch the smoky cloth. When a man comes from the club smelling like smoke, he hopes the woman will say, "Ooh that smoke stinks, you need to go in there and take a shower." Well, that's the man's cue to go take a shower after messing around with another woman without the shower being obvious to the woman.

A woman can catch him if she says, "You don't smell strong like smoke like you usually do." My ex-wife got me like that. From then on, I kept cigarettes in the car just to blow smoke on my clothes. I would spray a little water on me and then blow smoke on my clothes so I could have that smoky smell and I would gargle with a little alcohol so she would think I was out all night partying. Women are smarter!!!!

## 99.9 PERCENT

Men are not to blame all the time. Some women are straight disrespectful and outright shameful. They have a plan of attack when they go after young guys who play professional sports with big contracts. They want to get pregnant by him to get that big permanent monthly check.

Even more scandalous, young ladies get pregnant by what I call foul play. Here's how: The man is using a condom for protection because he doesn't want any kids with her. She takes the used condom and puts it in the freezer, then gets it injected into her vagina later on. After nine months, she goes to court and is able to prove that the baby is his because the blood test is 99.9 percent positive. Now she gets paid for the next eighteen years.

Who is she really cheating? The child! She played the man and no one can be mad at the brother because that's some seriously tricky stuff. Stop blaming everybody and start blaming yourself; get off the path of blaming and get on God's path to healing.

We each have a purpose in life and I think this mission of informing and protecting women is mine. The sooner you figure out what yours is, the happier you'll be.

## WOMEN PLAY GAMES TOO

Quit playing games. She lets a man come over, feeds him a good home-cooked meal. She gets all touchy teasing, he gets on top of her, rolls until he gets the big bulge, then she sends him home.

That's playing games. She should just be grown. If she's going to go that far, she should go ahead and make a night of it. If she likes him enough to invite him over and prepare dinner for him, just know that in a man's mind he's saying "We're going all the way." All that rolling round and foreplay, then rejection—that isn't really foreplay for men.

## DATING GAMES: LET'S TURN THIS AROUND

Don't spend quality time with unqualified people. When you find a man you like well enough to date, stop playing games.

Something major must happen to turn this whole thing around. I think until we all start respecting one another, it's going to be a long wait, because as we grow up and young kids see us doing these things to one another, they're going to do it too.

The kids modify some of these same habits in their relationships to fit their needs, and of course that makes it worse. The result is a cycle of disrespect between men and women. So now you can see why I say that we're going to have to join in and kick this respect thing off and turn this whole relationship thing around.

# Six

# GOD WILL GET YOU!

*God gives us blessings. If we abuse our blessings, they are taken away.*

I had a really good job before I started using women to make a living. I ran my own business and was making quite a bit of money. I also worked as a bodyguard making a very nice salary.

The company I was contracted with was sued by a big oil company and went out of business. I happened to be married at that time and lost my business and several employees. During that time my wife left me, and the man who I was a bodyguard for died in a car accident—all of this happened in the same month.

Before any of these things happened I remember promising God that if He would let me get a big contract I would go to church, quit partying, and stop cheating on my wife.

God answered my prayers, and once I got the big contract I bought more clothes, partied more, stayed out later, acquired a lot more women, and didn't go to church for six or seven years. I told myself I didn't have time for church. All I had time for was more women.

I'm pretty sure all the bad things that happened to me were some of God's work. He brought me back down and made me humble because I broke the promises I made to Him. Be careful of the promises that come out of your mouth when asking God for help because you might have to stand up and pay up!

## IT'S NOT BROKE IF SHE CAN FIX IT

Women try so hard to find that special man. They pray to God for the right man, and then they keep going into situation after situation with the wrong man. A woman has to first *create* the kind of man she wants in her mind, then she can *prepare* for the man to enter her life. What a woman sees doesn't always come true, but what a woman believes does.

I'm pretty good at repairing, fixing, and building things, such as houses, mirror designs, or just adding on to structures, so I think in craftsman terms. We men have a little saying: *"It's not broke if I can fix it."* I want women to do the same thing in their lives.

A woman keeps hollering that somebody broke her heart, but she knows how to fix it, so it isn't really broke. Just repair it and move on. The longer you are angry with a person for hurting you, the longer you allow that person to control you.

Imagine this: The woman puts a hole in the wall or maybe her kids did it. Now all she has to do is call the Sheetrock guy. He'll put a patch over it, putty it, tape it, and paint it and it will look like it was never damaged. She can do this with her life too. She should know that what somebody has broken can be fixed.

All she has to do is holler out to God and He'll fix it for her. But no, she walks around wanting the man back, thinking that's going to fix it. Sometimes she will even go shopping and buy new clothes or she tries to find another man and think that's going to fix it.

If it isn't broke, she can't fix it, and if it gets broke and she leaves it broke, it's because she doesn't know how to fix it or doesn't want to fix it. She wants to stay angry and broken. The next time a woman's relationship gets broken she should ask herself several questions:

1. Is this worth fixing?
2. Does he deserve a second chance?
3. Do I really want to go through this mess?
4. What's the likelihood of this happening again?
5. Is it worth the heartache and pain?
6. Have I lost my mind?

Remember, there is nothing new under the sun. If it's happened to you, it has happened to another woman and she has gotten through it—you can too.

## GOD GIVES IT TO US IN TIME
God gives us what He wants us to have when He's ready for us to have it. If He gives it to us before time, we won't be able to keep it because we won't know what to do with it. God has His seasons; be prepared for yours.

I know He gives in time because it has happened to me. I had to wait for my season to come.

## A GOD-GIVEN GIFT
I want to talk a little about a woman's God-given gift. So many women try to decorate their outside before they fix the inside.

Have you ever driven around in December and seen the Christmas decorations all lit up on the houses and in the yards? But you never see the gifts on the outside of the house. All the gifts are on the inside of the house under the tree.

It's the same with a woman; her gifts are on the inside. She needs to reach inside, pull them out, and share them accordingly.

The preacher said, "Sometimes you miss the blessing behind you; now don't turn around and miss the ones in front of you."

# Seven

# REAL WOMEN — REAL ISSUES

*The best way to bring out the man in a man is for a woman to be more of a woman.*

If a woman puts as much time into finding God as she does into finding a man, she will realize God created her and knows how great a person she is. She will definitely understand that God also knows what type of man she needs. In the Bible it says, "He who finds a wife finds a good thing."

Because God created woman, He won't mind sharing this woman with another great person that He created. God helps direct women, therefore letting the right man into her life.

## ASKING GOD TO SEND A MAN
A woman gets to me when she starts asking God to send her a good man. Then she starts describing what kind of man she wants God to send. Women will say things like, "I want me a man that's a roughneck. I want a man with a little hardness in him." "I don't want an easygoing guy.

A woman should start thinking more about what she's asking

God. Why doesn't she just ask God to send a man with a godly heart instead of a man that's a little hard? She should let God do what He does best—and send her the right man.

## WHAT SHE LOVES ABOUT THE MAN

It's not one particular thing about a man that makes a woman love him. It might be something that stands out about him that makes her like him more. Because love is unconditional, whatever it is she loves about him is because of the love she has for him.

A woman should write down five things she loves about her man. Once she writes them down she should post them on a mirror so she can see it daily. Maybe she won't be so quick to forget why she loves him when she gets angry or when they're going through rough times.

## WOMEN ARE COMPETITIVE

Competition is strong among women. No woman ever wants to lose to another woman, period. She doesn't care how bad things get with her man; she will stay with him and take mistreatment just to feel like she won against the other woman and show her that "You can't take *my* man." She will take verbal abuse, emotional abuse, and even physical abuse just to prove she can win. No matter how bad the man is treating her, how much money he's spending on the wrong things, or how little he cares about her, she will stay as long she thinks she can win the man. That's not right!

When a man is mistreating a woman she should write his name on a piece of paper and throw it in the trash. Then recite *"Trash in, trash out of my life."* That should be her motto from that point forward. When she's being treated badly she should realize that he's not her man any longer, nor the man she should be with. She should find something positive about herself that she can love and find the strength to give herself better love.

## WOMEN HAVE GAME

If guys knew what I know, they could learn how to get more women when they're not trying.

You see, a woman will chase a man when she sees that he doesn't want her. Actually, a man sees the woman as soon as she walks in the door. He sees her looking at him, but when he looks back at her she turns away. When he looks away she looks at him and when he catches her looking at him again, she acts as if she didn't even see him. Like I said, "Women have game." Men see right through it. So just work on being yourself.

## SLICK MOVES AT THE BAR

Even though the waitress comes to the table to serve a woman drinks, she will get her behind up and go to the bar and order a drink because she knows the man sitting at the bar will say, "Hey, I'll pay for that."

Women have some pretty slick moves. If a man doesn't notice the woman, she'll say something innocent to get his attention. She'll even say things like, "Excuse me, can I get through to order a drink?" Women have all kinds of game.

## FIGHTING MAKES HIM LOSE RESPECT FOR HER

It amazes a man when a woman fights so hard for him and he's not even showing her that he wants her. It makes him reject her even more and he slowly loses respect for her.

If a woman is going to be intimate with a man, it should be on her terms and with a man who cares for and respects her. A woman should not waste her time with a man who doesn't respect her, because men don't like women who will let men run over them. They consider her weak by this time.

If a man shows disrespect for a woman, belittles or abuses her, doesn't open up his personal life to her, doesn't spend quality time with her, and doesn't desire her, she should close her legs and move on with her life.

When a woman can feel that the man has lost feelings for her, she has got to close her legs and end it. She has got to love herself more than this. Don't wait for him to tell you it's over, when you know it's over. Don't be afraid to move on to something better.

## DEMAND RESPECT FROM MEN

There's a certain way a woman can demand her respect from a man and mean it. If he approaches her, there are certain things she can do to let him know he shouldn't cross a certain line.

Your body language is a great aid to helping you get respect from a man. Carry yourself like a real first lady. There's also a certain way you can stand when he says something. Don't give off sexual body language early. You can also give him the cold-heart treatment and make him feel like he's nothing or you can ignore him completely. He'll know he has to work to get you.

The best thing to do is give him the cold shoulder by acting real cool about him. If he's trying to say something funny to make you laugh, you can do a half laugh. You can keep a straight face and say, "Oh yeah, that's funny." There are certain things a woman can do to let a man know he has to stop messing with her because she's not trying to play games. If he asks for your phone number, take his; stay in control from the beginning.

## Women Should Not Criticize Other Women

A woman should not criticize or talk about other women in negative ways. If a woman must talk about another woman, it should be something positive. When she's saying good things, no one can confront her later about it. If you build one another up, you'll have a strong group of confident women and men can't easily use you as prey for their selfish needs.

Talking negative is messy and mess has a tendency to cause more mess. Besides, a woman should have better things to do with her time and her mouth than tear down another diamond.

## Negative 411 About a Man

When a woman is told something about the new guy she's dating, she should not immediately ask him about it. She should take the information she has and put it away in her mental database and simply keep an eye on the situation. The truth will eventually come to light. It always rears its head over time. All the woman has to do is remain mindful of what she's learned.

Don't give up on a man because someone told you something that you didn't like about him. It's okay to take advice and be mindful of what others are saying, but it's not good to turn your relationships upside down on the advice or forewarnings of others. Be sure to investigate the situation thoroughly. During your early dating stages your goal is to simply collect data to determine if this is a man you want to get to know better.

## Watch the Male Company You Keep

If a guy thinks the woman is a good woman and he's considering her, he'll watch her for a while. Once he sees her with a so-called bad boy, his thoughts of her being a good woman change.

Being associated with a nothing kind of guy turns men off. The potential partner now sees her in a negative way. He second-guesses whether he wants to be involved with her.

In reality, the woman may not be as bad as the potential partner thinks she is, but because of the company she keeps he doesn't want to take a chance on her. He thinks if a woman isn't that way, why is she with this bad boy? A woman should be careful of the company she keeps. A woman who hangs by herself is difficult to judge because no one knows what category to put her in and her chances of attracting a decent man are better.

## WATCH THE FEMALE COMPANY YOU KEEP
Men judge a woman by the female company she keeps too. A woman can run with a nice group of girls who are just not doing anything with their lives, and because they are her friends she doesn't see any reason not to hang with them.

A man looks at the kind of women she's hanging with and he'll put her in the same category as them. If they act wild and sleazy, he assumes she is wild and sleazy too. If they present themselves as a conservative group of women, he will naturally assume she is conservative too. When a woman is trying to get a man it's okay for her to roll solo.

## ARE YOU THE COMPANY HE KEEPS?
A woman shouldn't get caught up in looking for a man who has everything because it will be difficult to have him to herself. If he's an older gentleman and he's tired of looking around, he might settle for only one woman, but if he's a younger man, he wants to sow his oats and get all the sex he can before he settles down. It's kind of hard for a woman to have a *younger* man all to herself when he has

plenty of money and doesn't need anything except the company of a woman.

In reality all she ends up being is part of his heavy rotation. If she's lucky enough to have a man who wants her, she's found the needle in the haystack. If misery loves company—what is she doing in his house? Being company! Enough said. So be realistic and keep your legs closed and get the facts before sharing your emotions.

## LAY DOWN SOME RULES

A woman has got to have the strength and sense to let the man know what she will and will not tolerate. She has to do this in the beginning, middle, and end of the relationship. If a woman never gives a man any rules about what she expects or wants from the relationship, how will he know what hurts her, what she will tolerate, what she appreciates, or how she wants him to communicate with her?

I'll call this a "how-to" package. She should tell him how to please her the most. If he continues to do something against her wishes, then she has something to gripe about. She cannot gripe at a man when he doesn't know the reason. She has to open up and talk to him. She has to lay down some ground rules in the very beginning of the relationship! He won't have a clue if she doesn't give him any.

## SOMETIMES A WOMAN ISN'T ALL THAT

I have a friend who's forty-two years old and she's found a good man. He's a God-fearing and hardworking man, but the only problem is he's green, meaning he doesn't know much about relationships with women.

She says she's tired of teaching him everything. Because I know this woman and her history with men, I would say that in her forty-two years of looking, it appears she's the one who hasn't learned a thing. If she's the one who knows everything, why can't she keep a man?

Maybe when she starts teaching her man what it is she likes, she might learn something about herself. She'll also learn that she isn't the complete package she thinks she is.

Women should stop thinking they are so fine and so cute that any man should feel lucky to have them. No matter how fine a woman is, somewhere out there there's somebody who's tired of her.

## YOU CAN DO BAD ALL BY YOURSELF

When a woman meets a man who has never been married and he has no children, she should realize that there are reasons why he's in that situation. There are exceptions to every rule, but if the man is over forty years old, has never been married, and doesn't have children, it's often because his priorities are out of order.

A woman should really question this kind of man. He'll usually say, "I'm going through a divorce," "I'm breaking up," or something of that nature. He's always got an excuse for why he's doing badly. Nothing ever changes. He's usually lying to himself to get over on the woman. If a woman fools with this guy she's in for heartache, pain, and suffering. Hold off till he gets himself together.

## WHEN A GOOD MAN CHEATS

A woman cannot get something for nothing, not even a man. When she's looking for a man, it's difficult to find one who has never done anything wrong. It's difficult to get a man who won't look at other women or chase after other women, unless you meet a man who has sold out to God and doesn't let his urges overtake him.

If a woman gets a man who does everything for his family and there is no appreciation for his efforts, he soon gets tired of doing everything and wants out or wants to find someone who makes him feel appreciated. He even wants to get away from the woman he once loved. He puts her on his list of things to get rid of.

The man might be a good man, but when he gets a chance or opportunity to have an affair, he takes it. That becomes so much fun he doesn't want to stop.

So now he's messed around with another woman. He'd been a good man so far but made one mistake. Does she just throw him away? She knows he still loves her and she still loves him, but does she still get rid of him?

In order for a man to prove his love for a woman and show her that he won't make that mistake again, he should do something extraordinary that she'd like. He might try these things first:

- Go to counseling.
- Change his phone number.
- Leave his cell phone on twenty-four hours a day and let her answer it.
- Make sure that she always knows his whereabouts.
- Answer the phone anytime she calls him, even in meetings, and say he'll have to call her back if necessary.
- Be available to her twenty-four hours a day.
- Check in with her throughout the day.
- Show his love in more romantic ways than one.

Everybody slips up in different ways every now and again. It might be you the next time. So ladies, make sure your man feels appreciated. If he's a good man and he's trying, remember nobody is perfect—not even you.

## THREE KINDS OF WOMEN

A man usually has three different categories he puts a woman in when he meets her. They are:

1. The one-night stand. He doesn't care about her and just wants to hit it.
2. The undercover lover. He will date or sneak around with her, while hoping that no one sees them together. You never really get introduced to his inner circle.
3. The wife material. He wants to marry her someday.

Which one are you?

## THE CINDERELLA SYNDROME

Some women desire love so bad that they will compromise pride, family, and self-esteem for the white picket fence and the little swing in the yard.

I don't know when it started, but the "Cinderella Syndrome" has been brainwashed into a woman's head since she was a little girl, and now she thinks it's the law—as if that's the way it's really supposed to be. Wake up! You have got to be realistic about love, your expectations, and relationships.

## WOMEN WILL GO THE EXTRA MILE TO GET A MAN

When a woman finds a man who only has one of the qualities she requires, she gets so excited that she starts planning her life around him. She cooks him dinner, washes his clothes, takes care of his children, and even puts his picture on her desk—all before he deserves it. She does all of this before she even knows who he is, what he likes, or what he wants in a woman and his future. It's as if she goes into get-a-man mode.

Women have got to get to know the man before they start the marathon to really get him. Women will go an extra mile to get a man even before they know whether he wants her. Slow down, take a deep breath, and think before you leap.

## WOMEN TAKE MEN ANY KIND OF WAY

A man doesn't ever lie down. He's always trying to get higher and many times he does it through a woman. Sometimes a woman doesn't care what shape her mind is in. If a man can fool her enough to make her think that he's somebody or if he can make her think she has it going on, she will take him—any kind of way. Just to say, "I have a man."

A woman will take a man even with baggage. He's taking care of his parents. She takes him even though his wife has left him and he has three or four kids to care for. Even if the man has eight cats and nine dogs, it doesn't make a difference. Once she commits to him she comes right on in and starts feeding the cats and dogs, changing dirty diapers on grown folks, and feeding those kids and combing their hair.

But what if the shoe is on the other foot. Let her mama get sick while he's dating her. He starts finding ways to get out of the relationship. Now, if she thinks the man will marry her, she will go so far as to reject her own mother. The man starts saying, "Why don't we put your mama in an old folk's home." He immediately starts asking questions . . . "Are all these kids yours? How old are they? Don't any of them want to stay with their daddy?" He continues to say things like, "Look here, I don't like cats. I don't like dogs!" So now she has to get rid of all her pets!

But the killing thing about it is that for love—or the illusion of love—the woman will get rid of all she loves to please that man. Women can be crazy like that!

## SHE WANTS HIM AND THAT'S OKAY

There are some women who set out to find a man—any man. No matter what it takes to do it, she does it. She lets the man know she's interested in him and if he starts a conversation with her, he can say anything to her—good or bad—and she wants him.

If the woman lets the man know she's interested in him, he can respond by saying anything to her and it'll work. Sometimes the man doesn't even care about the woman. All he wants is the chance to get her in bed.

The only prerequisite for the man is that the woman *wants him*. That's enough to get the communication going in the right direction. When he begins to talk to her he finds out whether she is easy to get in bed or challenging.

If she's easy, he pursues her. If she's not, he might still pursue her, but only to get her in bed. It's best for you women to stay in control of whether he deserves you or not. Don't just fall prey for the feel-good at the moment.

## WHAT MAKES A WOMAN LAUGH CAN ALSO MAKE HER CRY

During those first happy moments when a woman meets a guy and she's sitting with him, having drinks, conversation, and laughs, she thinks he's a great guy.

A woman could keep herself from feeling unnecessary pain if she doesn't have sex with him before she does research on him. All that laughing will make her cry if she doesn't keep her senses and find out about him before she gets involved with him. Don't let those butterfly feelings take over you too soon.

## WHEN A WOMAN HAS HAD ENOUGH

When a woman finally stops putting up with a man's "I need to be me" attitude and tries to stand up for herself, she can tell the man she's not going to take it anymore.

Because she took a stand, he begins to put her out of his life and starts cheating on her. He adds a new relationship with another woman and that creates more instability, which causes more hell in the household. Don't stay around and tolerate this. If he wants to have multiple relationships and that's not your thing, keep those legs closed and bring closure. Women: enough is enough. Stand up for yourselves.

After five or six months, the man is expecting the woman to leave, and if the woman doesn't leave, he tries to do something to make her leave so he can be left alone. He often considers the woman to be in his way and will try to make her take the blame. He gets another unassuming woman who doesn't know about him or his past. The man ends up having seven to ten women at the same time. That way he always has somewhere to go or someone to make him feel like he's the man.

Now, if a woman doesn't like how he does things, she is free to leave and he doesn't care because he has more women waiting as his backup. In reality this kind of man needs some of these women to leave, but he never tells any of them this. He waits on the woman to mess up so it's her fault the relationship ended. Then he can always stop by and have "I'm sorry sex" with her.

When a woman thinks she's the one who messed up, she's vulnerable and leaves the door open for a second chance. Because she feels this way the man is never to blame—so he thinks. So ladies, when you've had enough—end it.

## WOMEN PUT UP WITH TOO MUCH MESS
I'm glad there are women out there who don't want problems in their home, but it's bothersome when a woman goes along with something just to get along with the man. It's best she finds another way to make her home happy.

There's nothing like living in an uncomfortable situation and oftentimes the woman is living in one. She's unhappy at work and she's unhappy at home. She stays with her job because she doesn't want to change jobs and because there's nothing else for her to do, but when she's home that's supposed to be where she can relax and let everything go. But she can't because her home is worse than her job. She'd rather be at work, but she loves that man so she keeps him and she keeps living and dealing with a situation she hates. Why?

## WOMEN WHO HAVE MORE THAN ONE MAN
If a woman wants a real relationship, but is currently dating two or more men, she should select the one who has most of the qualities she likes in a man She should feel comfortable with choosing a man who's compatible with her.

Two's a couple, three's a crowd, and more than that's a party. If the woman is dating one man, she should pay close attention to him because it could affect the rest of her life.

## MEN WHO HAVE MORE THAN ONE WOMAN
When a woman dates a man who's dating more than one woman, someone is getting cheated. When she finds a man who needs more than one woman in his life, neither she nor the other woman is get-

ting her fair share. If he has several other women on the side she knows that he's not her man; he's not anyone's man.

## INVOLVING OTHER PEOPLE

If the woman confides in a man she should be careful not to fall for him just because he understands and has been helpful. The man she is confiding in is very understanding, attentive, and willing to help. She feels that he is able to see it from her point of view and now she has a shoulder to lean on. When this happens, he soon becomes the *idea* man who she wishes could be the *ideal* man.

If a woman thinks that the man she is confiding in is the one she wants to be with, she should think it through and ask herself, "Could I live with this person if I had to?" Most times the answer is no. She should also ask, "Can he live with me?" Remember, he's just getting the woman's version of the situation. If she wants him to move in after a week or two, the man might think, "This woman is crazy."

## CONTINUE TO IMPROVE WHO YOU ARE

A woman should never stop working on self-improvement. If all of a woman's past relationships have failed in the same way, chances are she's the problem.

If she involves other people who she can trust, she should make sure she tells them the whole truth. One half the truth only gets one half the solution. She shouldn't confuse others' opinion of the situation with her own feelings.

## USE COMMON SENSE

Sometimes all a woman needs is common sense. It can take her further in life. If a woman tries to go through life without an education, and tries to get the finer things in life, but doesn't use common sense, she will end up living a life of poverty.

This same woman could end up pushing a carriage with some blankets in it and trying to find a place to sleep. A woman *must* use her common sense above all else.

## TRY NEW THINGS

It's important that a woman *not* be afraid to try something new. She should try different things in her life to see what works.

Trying new things can help a woman understand that her life is open to more opportunities. A woman who explores different opportunities and tries new things will automatically bring new accomplishments into her life.

## A WOMAN IS AT LEAST 50 PERCENT TO BLAME

No woman is going to throw away the perfect man. If he's half as good as he makes himself out to be, women will be willing to fight for him. No one should take the blame or give all the blame for the destruction of the relationship. Both people carry at least 50 percent. Remember, it takes two.

## IT TAKES TWO

No matter how good they look to the public, nearly all relationships have problems. They may be big or small, but it's happening. Why? Because anytime you take two humans and join them as one, someone won't know how to count. In other words, at least one person in the relationship will mess up. Problems are bound to arise, especially if somebody doesn't know how to count.

Aargh, remember, it takes two.

## THE VENUS AND MARS THEORY

When a woman hears people saying that men are from Mars and women are from Venus, that simply means there are two sexes from two different planets trying to live together right here on earth. I say men are from the East Side and women are from the West Side.

Many times we find couples struggling with how to deal with each other and they can't even handle earth; now Mars and Venus are thrown in the picture.

## KNOWING IF HE'S THE RIGHT MAN

A woman's heart will help her determine if she has the right man. Having a talk with God will help too. A woman should never be afraid to ask God if her man is the man God has sent to her. A woman should not allow her head, or her tail, to dictate if he's the right one. When a woman encounters the right man, she will know. When she is comfortable and feels secure with this man, she can start deciding if he is right for her. When he tells her he is ready to settle down, remember that his actions will speak louder than words.

## WHAT EVERY WOMAN SHOULD KNOW

There are a few things men really wish women would do. For example, when a woman is simply hanging around her home at the conclusion of her date, she should continue to wear her heels. Heels make everything about her look good to the man. Her legs look better, her butt looks tighter, and her man is in awe.

She should not take her heels off nor put on her flats or house shoes. She should not walk around barefoot in her stockings when she's trying to impress a man. She usually has no idea how bad her butt looks after taking her shoes off. Her butt drops and is not up in the air anymore. Now the man is looking at the woman thinking, "What happened to the butt." A woman should be careful of her barefoot presentation. You lose points early; you might go from a 100 to an 89.

A woman should try to keep her shoes on until it's time to take them off, like when it's time to go to bed or make love. The rule: keep the heels on while standing. If she is sitting she can take them off, but when she stands she should put them back on. A woman in heels is sexy to a man.

## WOMEN ALLOW MEN TO MOVE IN TOO SOON

I feel bad for the kids, the little girls and the little boys in the house, when a woman has a grown man coming in there and she doesn't even know who he is or where he comes from. Before she moves a man in with her she should ask herself:

1. Has he been locked up for child molestation?
2. Does he have any cases pending?
3. Does he have any past child abuse cases?
4. Does he even like children?
5. Does he have children of his own?
6. Has he ever hurt any children?

A woman will think so much about her own needs that she allows new men to come into her house for all the wrong reasons. Now this grown-ass man is looking at her daughter and/or her son in sexual ways and she's too blind to notice it.

The woman brings him into her home because she's trying to fulfill her sexual needs, but he's not looking at her all the time. He's looking at her children every chance he gets. Too many women are guilty of exposing the wrong man to their innocent children. He's making overt comments about the sexual parts of her children's bodies and she's so into him that she chooses to be blind to his real reasons for being there.

To get even closer to her children and manipulate her mind he insists that the woman go out on the town and he'll babysit the children. And guess what? She goes out and leaves her children with a man she's known for a very short period of time. He's left with her children to do as he pleases. Women, do not take chances with your children; they are innocent and they depend on you. Spend some time with that man, his friends and family, and know his environment before you trust him with your children.

## SHACKING UP

Let's discuss the lady who's been shacking with a man and he's still trying to figure out if he wants to marry her. I'm not saying it's right for a woman to shack up before she gets married, but she sure can find out some things about the man when she does it. And those things can help her before she considers marriage. After she finds out a few things she might get married anyway and find a way to deal with them, but it's the things she won't know about him that are going to shock her.

Even if everything is going fine in the relationship, shacking up with a man is not good. If she's getting along with him there are probably other things happening in her life that would be going better if she wasn't living in sin. If she does the right thing and says, "I do," things will be better than they are now.

Maybe she'll wait to get married. Who really knows what a woman will do. My wife and I have been married about three years and she'll say to me, "You're crazy," and I'll say, "You knew that before we got married." And then she'll say, "*No* I didn't either, but

I'm married to you now and I love you, so I'll find a way to deal with it."

The only real reason a man waits to marry a woman is because she lets him wait.

## WOMEN WHO CLAIM TO BE GOOD WOMEN

Sometimes women will foolishly say, "I haven't ever did anything wrong; I'm a good woman." If a woman really thinks she has never done anything wrong, then she is foolish!

A woman should admit her mistakes. Everyone makes them and needs help at one time or another. Admit it, work on it, and improve it, but don't tell the lie and say you've never done anything wrong. She should stop thinking that it's all about her.

## SHE'S THE ONLY ONE IN HER WORLD

Many times a woman's world seems so big to her because she's the only one in it. If she allows others to come into her world, it will become smaller and she can face her issues better. People are willing to help if they are allowed, but the woman has to open up and welcome others into her world.

## SOME MEN FEEL THAT BLACK WOMEN ARE DUCKS AND WHITE WOMEN ARE SWANS

Even in the pimp world, black women are disrespected more than white women. This is not a put-down, just facts.

Men have an old saying: "Black women are ducks and white women are swans." Even though both are selling their bodies, they are placed in different categories.

The pimps say, "When you got a duck you got bad luck." In the pimp world black women are known for keeping mess going. They hide the money, jump on the other girls at the drop of a hat, and talk trash all day long. So sisters, quit low-rating yourself and let's try to upgrade. Don't lighten up . . . tighten up.

## SOME WOMEN ARE REALLY STRONG

It's amazing how strong some women really are and don't even know it. Women are very strong. They have babies, take care of the children, work all day, keep the house clean, run the errands, and cook the meals, just to mention a few.

The man pays the bills and for that he thinks he's not supposed to do anything else. He sits back and watches TV and then says he needs a night out with the boys.

When a man gets bored he looks for other women. When a woman gets bored she looks for other projects.

## HER HEART CAN OVERRULE HER MIND

The thing that makes a woman weak is her heart; because once the heart is capable of loving a man it makes women second-guess themselves. A woman's heart overrides her mind when she is emotionally connected to a man even though she knows he's the wrong guy for her.

The first thoughts she thinks are real, but her heart usually kicks in and says, "No, it's not that way." Her heart tells her to accept things that she would not normally accept. She loves him, but her mind is trying to figure out what to do because now the bad is starting to feel good.

## GOD WILL PROTECT A WOMAN'S HEART

A woman tries to gain strength until she can handle her business. God holds her heart, and if she prays before she goes into battle her heart will be protected.

## CONSISTENTLY IMPROVE YOURSELF

A woman should take time to work on herself and try to improve in all areas of her life. When it's time to select a man she'll have the ability to get more of the man than what she could have gotten.

## A WOMAN WILL SAVE A MAN BEFORE
## SHE SAVES HERSELF

I've seen women that will save a man before she tries to save herself. I have seen women rob banks with men and let men talk them into doing wrong. I've seen women go to jail for men they love so much that they don't want to see them locked up.

The woman decides to do the time so the man can stay out on the streets and make money. And that works sometimes, but most times he has another woman while she's in jail doing his time. If she had taken that same energy and decided to do some time with God, she could have been doing good time. With all the strength a woman has, she still believes that it's hard to be what she wants to be and it's easier to be what she doesn't want to be.

## WOMEN FAKE THE FUNK

Women try to play tough around their friends. They say things like, "Let him leave, I don't care." "Girl, I'm not thinking about him." Then when their friends have gone—they cry.

I'm still trying to figure out why a woman takes herself through that. Even though she loves the man, she plays tough and comes up on the short end. The man starts believing she really doesn't care and he moves on. When she sees him with another woman she loses it, she has a fit.

Express your relationship from a positive point of view. Leave the negativity out and live with him in the most positive way. Remember, the woman was the one who said, "Let him leave." Women, say what you want from the man. Don't play games with your own emotions, because at the end of the day, the joke is played out at your own expense.

## KEEP YOUR BUSINESS TO YOURSELF

When a woman sees her man with her girlfriend, she's ready to fight and badmouth her, but if she had kept her business to herself and stopped talking so much about what was going on in her relationship, her friend might not have him. Yes, a friend will give opinions, advice, and criticisms, all in your favor, but she's also listening to what you say is good about him. She's taking notes from all you say. Remember, the very things you're complaining about might be the things your single friends like about him. Stop telling your girlfriends about your man and your sex life.

If a woman tells her man how good he is instead of telling her girlfriends, he might be able to make things better. A woman might not tell her man that his love is good, but when she talks to her girlfriends she expresses jubilation, ecstasy, and satisfaction. Now her girlfriends are looking at him like he's a piece of steak. They are ready to eat him as soon as she turns her back.

If the woman tells the man how good he is, he might bring her even more goodies and some extra special delights. A woman cheats herself when she tells her girlfriend and not her man how good he is.

## WOMEN SHOULD FIND TIME TO LISTEN

When a woman finds a guy who brags on himself and tries to tell her everything about himself, she should not interrupt him. She should not try to outtalk him or make statements that cause him to think she doesn't want to hear it. She should listen to everything he has to say.

She should listen with her ears and not her mouth during this time. She should remain quiet and try to understand what he's talking about. He might open up and tell her something about himself that she really needs to know. He might help her decide if he's the man for her. He might even give her great warning signs, if she's quiet and listens.

## Single Women

Single women are sometimes miserable, very opinionated, and usually wish they had a man. There are many women who wait on some woman to throw her man out so they can go get him.

When a woman is having problems in her relationship she should stop asking single women what she should do. They are the wrong people to ask.

## Living Alone

If a woman is single and lives by herself, she's a target for any man who's looking for a place to stay. A man knows if she lives alone and thinks he won't have to pay for a hotel. He'll feel that he always has somewhere to go. He'll stop off at her home; do what he has to do with her, and then he'll get out of there.

When a woman suggests to a man that they go to his place and he hesitates by saying, "Well . . . um . . . ah we can, but ah . . . let's try it tomorrow . . . maybe . . . I got something to do . . ." and making all kinds of excuses, she might want to think twice about him. A lot of men don't have their own place. They still live with their mama or some other girl.

A woman should make it a practice to check these things by researching him as if she's preparing for a college exam. If it were a test she couldn't write just anything on the paper when it was time to get her grade because her professor is not going to just give her any kind of grade. He's going to give her what she earned.

If she makes it a habit of treating her relationships like a test, she'll be obligated to put some time into studying the man inside out before she sleeps with him. She should have as much knowledge about him as she can. A woman can try her best to treat her life the same way. Look at it thoroughly before you cloud your head up with mess.

## WOMEN AND SURGERY ENHANCEMENTS

I'd like to speak on the subject of women who enhance their bodies with surgery, implants, and other things to improve their looks. As long as it helps them look beautiful, men see no problem with it. If a woman gets a man who doesn't like it, it's usually because he's insecure and doesn't want his woman to be beautiful just to keep other men from looking at her.

All that talk about "I like my girl natural"—don't believe him or let him put that on you. There isn't a man in the world who doesn't like a beautiful woman. Check that other guy out the next time; he's probably the one looking at everybody else's wife.

Whatever a woman does to make herself look better is great. She should feel free to do it and just let it go. She should do what she wants to do and what she has to do.

I'll never stop my wife from improving herself if it's going to make her look better and feel better.

## AVOID BECOMING HIS MOTHER

A woman cannot make a man think that she's trying to become his mama, even if he's a mama's boy. She shouldn't step over the *mama line;* instead she should work at being a good woman or wife and maybe even a best friend for him.

The biggest mistake a woman makes in a relationship is assuming the role of a man's mother. He doesn't need another mother; all he wants is for her to be his lady in public, his freak behind closed doors, and his best friend all the time. An older woman told me, "If you are not what you ain't, then you ain't what you are."

Women are trying to find somebody who has a last name they want and they haven't even figured out who they are or what their last name is yet.

# Eight

# A MAN

*Bringing old baggage into a new relationship can turn the new relationship into a long journey.*

A man learns how to be a womanizer by learning from other men—mainly his father. The more women he has, the better he gets at playing games. The better he gets at playing games, the more women he thinks will want him. The more women wanting him, the more he thinks he's the man.

After controlling a woman's mind for a while the man adds his own games and gimmicks to what he already knows and what he's learned from others.

## THE MAMA'S BOY

How do you know when he's a mama's boy? There are a few signs a woman can look for.

1. He takes her out to a nice restaurant and he's waiting on her to cut his food.
2. He gets ready for bed and she has to ask him if he's brushed his teeth.

3. He's not dressed right—asking her, "Baby, how does this look?" When he knows doggone well that jacket doesn't go with those pants.

4. He takes a drive with her and keeps asking, "Are we there yet?" "How much longer till we get there." "Are we almost there?" He should shut up and just ride.

If he's a mama's boy it'll be plain to see because his mama will come in his house and run it like it's hers and he won't stand up to her or say anything in his defense. The woman will be so tired of him she'll want to send him home with his mama. That's probably where the woman found him.

## Men Who Break Up with Women

It's amazing how possessive a woman acts with a man who breaks up with her. She's worse if she has kids by him. When the man leaves and gets another woman whom he loves and can get along with, the woman who he left becomes bitter. She was the one who didn't stand by him when times were hard and now she's angry.

When the man corrects some bad things in his life and moves on, the woman he left is angry because he didn't work to change these things while he was with her. His ex needs to quit hating on the new woman because the new woman did something the ex wasn't doing. The new woman probably showed him a different way to love and believed in him. Sometimes all it takes is something as simple as believing in him. And then again he moves on because some relationships are just not meant to be.

## Bringing Old Patterns into a New Relationship

A man is afraid to go back to a woman he mistreated. He automatically thinks she will hold a grudge if he cheated on her. To move forward she might forgive, but hopefully she'll never forget. She should never bring any bad feelings or grudges from an old relationship into her new one.

At first, I didn't understand why it was so important for a woman to bring newness into her relationship. It's as if she's taken old furniture from an old apartment and put it in her new home. The furniture probably won't look right or might even be outdated, but she puts it in there anyway.

I know, because that's what my ex-wife did. Instead of leaving old patterns and habits of her past relationship in the past, she brought them into our relationship and it created problems from the beginning. The woman's old baggage and the man's old baggage when joined together hurt the relationship. Sometimes the man is really trying to become someone new, but he and the woman aren't working from the same perspective. It destroyed our new relationship and that relationship is now my *old* relationship.

## A Woman Can Open a Man's Mind

When my new girlfriend, who's now my wife, said, "I'm here for you if you need me," I was afraid to get back with her because I thought she was going to say, "Don't try to run back to me because the relationship over there didn't work." But instead she said, "I'll be here if you need me." That small statement opened my eyes and made me wonder, "What kind of woman is this, who would still consider me after I made the wrong move?"

I was determined to find out more about this woman and I found out she was the kind I needed and wanted in my life. My eyes were opened to accepting someone brand-new. I suggest that a woman quit trying to date the same kind of man. Try something new, because the change might be better for you.

If a woman doesn't like a certain kind of man—shorter men,

heavy men, tall men, nerds, men with a little roughness—she should be willing to try something different. When a woman finds a man who's trying to change something about himself, she should start searching inside herself and see what she can also change. This change should be considered in order to help the new relationship work.

## GUYS DON'T WANT THEIR FRIENDS TO HAVE A WOMAN

If he has a woman in his life, his friends consider him trapped. If he is unavailable for fun and games and can't chase other women, his friends sometimes refer to him as being whupped or henpecked by the woman. A woman should understand that guys don't really want their buddies to have a woman. If he doesn't have a woman, he needs a running partner—a partner in crime, so to speak.

## FIND A WOMAN WITH QUALITY BEFORE THE NAME GOES ON

If a man wants to find a good woman he should go ahead and spend his *little-time money* and have *big-time thoughts*. He should find a woman with *little-time money* so if he ever gets any *big-time money* she'll still be there for him. If he ever has to come back to the little time she'll still be there for him. A man can find anybody to come in when he's big-time. To find a good wife a man has got to make sure the quality is there before his name goes on.

## MEN USE SHOCK VALUE

If a man can shock a woman he can get away with a lot of things because the woman won't believe it happened. He can shock her and before she knows it she's doing something she never really thought about doing.

I used to challenge women on the phone who said they weren't scared of me, and we would go back and forth: "No I'm not," "Yes you are," etc. I would tell her that she never had a big man before. As I drove toward her house I would talk my way into her seeing me at all hours of the morning.

As I arrived at the woman's house I would tell her that if she had on any clothes, by the time I got to the front door she should be buck naked. I would take off my clothes at the door. The woman would say, "What are you doing that for?" And I would answer by saying, "Why do you still have your clothes on? Why are you dressed?"

I would tell her that I knew we were thinking about the same things, so let's just go with it, and then we would have sex. She would give in to me and I would have her in the palm of my hand.

A woman should try her best to stay in control even when he uses shock value to get her to compromise.

## Men Are Like Dogs

If you don't give a man his freedom he can be like a dog. Imagine a woman who has a chain on a dog's neck in her backyard. The dog will run around the tree in a circle, but when the dog is unleashed and able to run free it's hard to catch. If the gate is open the dog shoots out and runs up and down the street.

That's kind of the way men are. If you don't give him his freedom he can be like a dog. A man loves his freedom, or at least the sense of having freedom. If you hold him on a leash, once he gets free he'll chase women hard, then go back home and act as if all is good, and allow his wife to put the chain back on his neck. All he needs is for his woman to give him a little freedom from time to time.

To get something that you never had, you have to do something that you never did.

## SEEING A WOMAN WITH ANOTHER MAN

I've had pain too. The finest woman in the world who I had ever seen at that time was my ex-wife. The greatest pain I ever felt was when I saw her in the arms of another man.

When another man has the woman you love you start seeing things about her that you never looked at before. You start asking yourself questions. You'll say, "She's been working out, hasn't she? Look at her legs. Her hair looks nice too." Men forget why they chose the woman in the first place, until she's with another man. What she is and what she has . . . it's been there all along, but most times men don't see it. They become so accustomed to seeing the woman on a daily basis that they've forgotten how good she looks and what she really looks like to other men.

## CHURCHGOING MEN

A woman should be mindful of the churchgoing man. Some men go to church just to be seen by women. That's their way of finding and getting women.

The man knows women tend to trust men who attend church. A woman is so proud to say her man goes to church that she ignores all the warning signs. He's sitting in church and hasn't heard a word the preacher is saying because he's looking around trying to find his next woman.

Every Sunday he's looking around the room trying to see where he's going to sit. When the preacher says hug your neighbor, he finds the woman he's scouted out and hugs her tighter and longer than the Christian greeting hug. The unassuming woman likes the hug and is now his potential prey. He now has her attention and moves in quickly.

If a woman keeps her eyes and mind open to the possibility that anything can happen, she'll understand that no one is perfect and she won't fall prey to predators, devils in disguise, or child molesters. Be careful of devils in disguise; they're in church too.

## PENITENTIARY MEN

Some women are really strange creatures. There's no limit to what they will or won't do for love. I know women who have waited on men who have been locked up for years. *Wait!* Now, every man in sight is coming after the woman. Guys with good jobs and good hearts too. Everybody who's anybody will come after her and she'll say, "Nah, I'm waiting on my man." He'll be out in ten more years. The woman will actually wait ten or fifteen years on a man, and as soon as the man gets out he has several other women.

The woman doesn't realize that no man wants to get out of the pen after being in there for ten or fifteen years and spend time with only one woman. He's got fifteen years of catching up to do. He wants to get what he thinks he's missed out on.

A large percentage of penitentiary men return back to the streets and try to screw around as much as they can to make up for lost time. The woman knows he can't make up for lost time, so she looks at *his* lost time as a way of being taught a lesson.

And there's a reason that it happened. It could be all for the good. But only God knows that. The strange thing about a woman is she'll wait for years, but if she catches him messing up she'll dump him the next week.

I'm trying to figure out why she can wait on a man who's been locked up fifteen years, but why can't she wait on God to send her a good man so she won't have to start back all over again.

## MEN'S COMMITMENT LEVEL IS CHALLENGED

Let's say a man's wife or main girl is doing time for him, so he doesn't get locked up. She gets ten years. No! Let's say she gets two years. She thinks he'll be sitting there waiting until she gets out? Oh, he could be sitting there waiting until she gets out, but he's going to have some on the side while he waits. Men just don't have the same level of commitment that a woman has for love.

Women think they do, but the stuff a man gives is much different from what a woman gives. A man gives a woman all he has, but it's still much different from the love a woman has for a man. You see, a man just loves, but a woman lives to love hard. She lives it, breathes it, and eats it. Just love is enough for a man.

## MARRYING MEN IN THE PENITENTIARY

It's amazing how a woman will marry a man in the penitentiary or a man on his way to the pen. That is absolutely crazy. No matter how much a woman loves a man, if she isn't married to him before he goes in, why would she marry him when he's on his way in, or already in? What's the purpose of a woman doing this? I think it's because she likes to say she has a husband, or maybe it's because she won't feel alone even though she is.

Women put their lives on hold for men all the time, but marrying a man in the penitentiary is considered the ultimate. Many times a woman is so confused by what love is that she doesn't really understand that she's putting her chance for a happy life on hold for months or years at a time.

A woman will often get lonely and have affairs on him. It happens all the time. Someone else might come along and sweep the woman off her feet and he might want to take care of all her needs, but she's sitting there lonely waiting on a guy who's probably going to do the same things when he gets out of the pen that got him in trouble in the first place.

Also the penitentiary man might not want the woman when he gets out. He might want a "him." A woman puts herself out of the dating game because she's desperate for a man, any man, and that's not good.

The woman's self-esteem has to be low when she marries a man in the pen. This marriage doesn't get him out of trouble, but it might get her into trouble. The woman will say, "At least he's not messing around on me." Ha, that's what a woman thinks. He may not be messing around on her the way she thinks, but he can still mess around with a man in the pen. It's called down low, because it's as low as he can go. (See Chapter 24.)

## MEN LOOK FOR WOMEN WITH LOW SELF-ESTEEM

When a man is at his lowest, he will reach and grab a woman who has lower self-esteem than he does. For example, an overweight girl with low self-esteem will take a man in—feed him, nurture him, pamper him, and love him. She will make sure he has food because she's going to always eat. An overweight woman is proud that she has a good-looking man—one who she can call her own—one who she will stand on her head and turn monkey flips for. Just to have a man to show off to her friends is considered an achievement for her.

People wonder . . . how, why, and when did all this happen? They ask one another, "Wow, what is he doing with *her*?" Or they say things like, "She must be paying him good to be with her." It's kind of like an old man with a young woman; the first thing people will say is, "He must be paying for her." They never think it's because of love.

This kind of relationship has occurred for centuries and I've had quite a few myself. I struggled all the way through them, but I always managed to live well because I had pride . . . because I was a showoff. I looked good, dressed well, ate well, and I was treated like a king by women. I demanded this. If I was down on my luck I looked for a woman with low self-esteem to land on.

## MEN WHO PICK ONE WOMAN OVER ANOTHER ONE

It's really just preference; it's what he likes. A woman should be careful of the way she lets a man punk her in front of her children. Two things can happen. I'll tell you what happened to me.

I watched my father raising hell all the time and I watched my mother be quiet most of the time because she didn't want to get into it with him. Her not wanting to get into it with him showed me that's what I'm supposed to do to shut a woman up. On the other hand it teaches daughters how to put up with unnecessary foolishness from their spouse.

So just be careful if you have to get into it with him. Go where the kids aren't around, and then address the situation. Remember not to discuss it in front of the kids; it damages them.

## WHAT A MAN LOOKS FOR IN A WOMAN

There are women who men consider their friend and are nice to them, but there's only one woman who can become his wife or the woman who he would be willing to put in his house. There are certain things a man looks for in a woman who he considers to be a special wifelike woman. She might have characteristics such as:

ladylike
sincerity
family values
a team player (doesn't mind helping out)
ability to blend in with his friend's wives
won't embarrass him in front of other women

She's the one he'll bring home to mama. The others he can let go without worrying or thinking about.

## WHAT HE DOESN'T LIKE

A man doesn't necessarily like for his woman to show all her skin when he first meets her. A woman showing her g-string after age thirty—I hope it's an accident. I can't speak for other men, but that's not cute. I think there should be a *draws law*. Men can always tell what kind of woman they are dealing with.

She can try to hide her true self, but it always comes out in the long run. He can tell if she's the kind of woman out there chasing men or whether she's a down-to-earth woman trying to live her life right. He knows if she wants a good life. She's the woman who doesn't play games.

## MEN STIR THINGS UP IN WOMEN

Imagine this scenario: a glass pot, a spoon, and a can of soup. Visualize the spoon as the man's private parts and the opening of the pot as the woman's private parts. She takes the can of soup, pours it into the pot, and stirs the soup. When she first looks at the glass pot all she sees is liquid on top, but once she stirs it up she begins to see the other ingredients that make the soup. The more she stirs, the more ingredients she sees floating to the top.

Looking at it from this point of view, it's the same thing that happens to a woman when she allows a man to penetrate her. He stirs up all her emotions until everything inside of the woman starts floating around and finally comes to the top.

Even when it's over, thoughts of him are still stirring around inside of her. As her emotions rise she begins to think about him more. She doesn't know which way to go or what to do. He has stirred up her emotions and there she is chasing him all over again. Many times a woman doesn't even know why she wants the man so bad. All she knows is she wants him. Sometimes women are just like soup.

## MEN ARE VISUAL: THEY ENJOY LOOKING AT WOMEN

A woman should understand that a man enjoys seeing her when she's looking good. He enjoys knowing that she is taking care of herself. He admires her looks and is proud to be a part of her life. She should not use the excuse of trying to be comfortable when she's looking her worst. To please her man and herself she might not be comfortable all the time, but she should know that pleasing her man takes effort—continuous effort. Another thing: a woman should look good, feel good, and be good to herself.

## MEN WANT A WOMAN WHO CAN BE REAL

A man likes to see a woman be real. She should simply be herself when a man meets her because most times he knows and she knows who she really is. She knows her limits and what she will and won't take. A woman should be herself and quit trying to fool people into believing she's someone else, because the man is going to find out later who she really is anyway.

The funny thing is, the person she's trying to be might not be the person he likes. If she had been herself from the beginning he might have liked her long before she pretended to be someone else.

## UNDERSTANDING WHY MEN DON'T CALL

Why do men just stop calling? They don't even call to tell a woman when the relationship is over. The man doesn't feel that he has to call because when he already knows it's over he feels that it's up to the woman to figure the rest out. Or he thinks that he shouldn't have to let her know it's over and believes he shouldn't tell her just in case he changes his mind and wants to come back later.

His other option is to simply tell her he was out of town or he was sick or he was going through some changes or he had some stuff on his mind. But guess what? She lets him right back in. He doesn't have to call because she falls for his lies every time.

## MEN DICTATE THE LENGTH OF A WOMAN'S HEALING PROCESS

The one thing that makes men sick is when the woman already knows it's over. She can catch him messing around with another woman, he'll watch her cry about it, let her be mad for two or three days, but no more than a week later he'll say to her, "Now that was last week, you need to stop all of this mess." He tells her that they're going to get this thing back together or else.

So now the man is trying to tell her how long her healing process should take, but just let him catch her doing something. He'll talk about it for the rest of his life. He won't let her out of it and he'll probably leave her. He can't see himself dating a woman who somebody else has been with while he's with her. He doesn't feel that he can take it and he doesn't know why she thinks he can take it. Men simply think women are stronger or bigger fools when it comes to these types of situations.

## MEN COULD LEARN A FEW THINGS FROM WOMEN

I used to watch women and hear them say, "I bet I can get him, girl. It's fun to me. It's just a game." He might want her and she might want him too, but she knows how to hold out.

I'm learning a lot just watching women. Watching women can help men learn, but they always want to be the ones out front trying to see how cold they are. They never really learn that the woman wants a man just as bad as a man wants a woman. She holds out longer because the man comes on stronger and faster. If the man never said anything to her, she could let him know that she wants him.

Ah, she can't wait to push upon the man and tell him how she feels. She wants to tell him what she would do if she were his woman and all that mess, but she sits back and waits before making a move. She's patient and manipulative. She waits for the right time to go after him. Men could learn a few things from women. Women don't mind waiting.

When a woman runs out there like a cabbage—all head and no tail—she's going to end up in the frying pan.

# Nine

# RELATIONSHIPS

*A relationship should feel as comfortable and as natural as farting.*

When a woman says, "Girl, he makes my heart skip a beat, and it goes pitty-pat," it might be fear trying to tell her to run. She'd better move her feet fast because in reality her brain is trying to tell her to run.

## RELATIONSHIPS SHOULD FEEL COMFORTABLE AND NATURAL

A relationship should feel good to both the man and the woman. The man wants to feel comfortable with the woman he has selected. He doesn't want to feel put upon or pressured in the beginning. If he feels pressured, he'll look elsewhere for peace. If it is to work, he should be allowed to be himself at any given time. The relationship should feel as comfortable and as natural to him as farting.

## A WOMAN SHOULD FEEL RELAXED

The woman should feel relaxed in the presence of the man whether she is in or out of bed with him. She shouldn't feel that she has to hide anything from the relationship.

When she's comfortable with him she can work out and not feel ashamed because she's sweaty and needs to bathe. She can eat in front of him or choose not to talk to him at all. If she wants she can lay up all day quietly in his presence and still feel that everything is okay.

A woman will have no problem being herself and acting herself when she's comfortable with her man. No airs, no fronts, and no false ideas of what a woman should be while with the man. She considers being able to be in her comfort zone with him a very important feature. She feels sure, alive, and happy! Men want their women to be this way.

## GIVE THE RELATIONSHIP A FAIR CHANCE TO WORK

A woman should be able to give her man a fair shot at making the relationship work. It's difficult for a woman to become familiar and understand a man if she keeps running back to her past relationships or taking advice from other people.

A woman should be able to stay and work things out when there are problems in the relationship. It's easy for a woman to run to another person when things are happening in the relationship that make her angry. She should not allow others to interfere when she's having problems in a relationship that she's trying to keep solid. She should give the relationship a reasonable amount of time to work.

## ALLOW THE MAN TO HELP RAISE HIS SON

If a man leaves a woman and his kids she should let him spend time with the kids, instead of trying to keep them away, especially if it's a boy.

A boy needs a man to help guide him in the proper direction.

It's not impossible for a woman to raise a man, but it is difficult. To make her job easier she should allow the father to at least spend quality time with the child. If it is so easy for a woman to make a boy into a man, why are so many women having problems with men? A woman doesn't even know where a man's problems lie, so she has trouble raising him. Maybe that was the same mistake she made with his daddy; she tried to make him into the man she wanted him to be and overlooked the man he really was. Even if the woman thinks less of the boy's daddy at least he can help the boy learn what it takes to be a man.

Allowing his daddy to help raise him will in turn help the women and assist the child in being the kind of man who treats women right. Also, allowing the son to grow up and be a man will help get our men back on track. Women can quit asking why men don't want to be men anymore.

A woman can't teach a boy what he needs to know about being a man, unless she wants him to grow up to be just like a woman, and I don't think anyone wants that!

## BRING SOMETHING TO THE RELATIONSHIP

A woman shouldn't bring a knife to a gunfight. If she brings a knife to the gunfight she won't win. She's not playing on level ground either. I'm not talking about a real knife or a real gun. I'm talking about a woman's time and worth.

It's similar to a relationship; when the man has something to bring to the relationship, the woman should bring the same thing. Women need to quit trying to go in relationships without bringing something to the table. They should stop looking for the man who already has everything. Bringing less to the relationship is like bringing a knife to a gunfight.

## TRY THE "POTLUCK" FORMULA

Maybe this thing can be broken down another way. When it's time to get together as a group, there's this thing called potluck, where everyone brings a different dish of food. The same goes for a relationship. She should bring something to the table, and then she can ask for different things. When she's trying to find a man who already has everything, she has to fall into his pattern. So she should look at it like potluck and bring her fair share to the table.

## DON'T PUSH TOO HARD

Women are trying to make their relationship work by pushing and pushing and pushing. My advice to women is don't sweat it. When a woman tries to force a relationship to happen, it doesn't work. Give him time and room and if it still doesn't work don't lighten up, but tighten up and close your legs.

## CHOOSING THE WRONG MAN CAN GET A WOMAN BUSTED

If the man is doing the wrong things to get ahead in life, when he gets busted the woman is going to get busted too. The house, cars, material possessions, and fabulous trips are all part of the illegal climb to the top if he's transporting illegal goods.

If the woman is caught with him, she'll go down with him and she's going to spend time behind bars. So when people say God bless the child that's got his own, that simply means every woman and man should have their own means of surviving.

A woman should not depend on a man to bring her total happiness. She should have her own means of survival and once she puts what she has with the man's it should be considered theirs. She's better off getting a relationship with someone who wants something out of life too.

A woman should not choose a man who has a short-term means of survival. She should ask him what his long-range plans are, then see what his answer is and check to see if he's working toward long-term stability. If his answer is unstable, then he's probably unstable. The woman should understand that he's probably a man moving in the wrong direction because most men who have real goals have a positive plan of action.

## TOO MANY WOMEN ARE TAKING OVER THE MAN'S ROLE

Some women try to take over the household and won't let the man be a man.

Too many women are taking over the man's role in the home so he's forced to take on the woman's role. Experimenting with changing roles often backfires on the couple. Some men cannot take the pressure women place upon them, so before they give up their manhood they decide to leave the woman. That's the demise of another relationship.

## GET A HANDY MAN AND STOP LOOKING FOR A BLING-BLING MAN

A woman should quit looking for the bling-bling and the money. There are good men out there who she's bypassing because she's trying to find the man with money. There are other men out there who are worth their weight in gold, are less expensive, handy with their hands, and can repair almost anything.

The one thing she can do is put some money into her house and find that man who's handy. He can move into her life and move out the rich guy because the rich guy won't ever be around. If she has a man who can repair things and is an all-around handyman, she can take the money they save and use it on other important things. When it comes to fixing a woman he can still be good with his hands. If she finds a man who's not handy with his hands and doesn't have a lot of money, she should ask questions that will help her decide if he's the right guy. She should ask:

1. Where has he been for the last ten years?
2. Is he still staying with his mama?
3. Does he have any kids?
4. Has he ever been married?
5. Is he married now?
6. Is he involved with any other women at this time?
7. What does he do for a living?
8. What are his future goals?
9. Did he finish school?

It's a long process trying to get a man where she needs him to be, but it can happen if the woman finds a man with some guts and some heart. It might take some time, but it can happen.

## TRY NOT TO BE TOO HARD ON EACH OTHER

Many men are raising themselves and going by the things that mama said, because mama was the only available parent. A woman should try not to be too hard on the guys.

There are things a woman can teach a man and a man can teach a woman, but each has got to find ways to do it.

It's not what you say, it's how you say it.

## THROWING AWAY A GOOD MAN

If he's a pretty good guy, a strong man, a God-fearing man, and he's paying the bills, and he messes up, the woman should think of him as somebody who simply slipped up a little.

If he's good for her and he's what she wants, she should give him another chance. Too many times the woman is ready to throw in the towel after the man makes one mistake.

Every man should be given at least one chance to mess up and two chances to get it right. A woman should always give a man the benefit of the doubt.

## TURN YOUR NEGATIVE ISSUES AROUND

You have to turn the negative relationship issues around by respecting each other. You don't have to always agree, but learn to agree to disagree. Remember, your kids are watching the things you do, and they will most likely repeat what you do, whether it's positive or negative. Wouldn't it be good to lay a positive path for you and them to follow? If they see a disrespect cycle, they will continue that unhappiness in their lives. Start having a loving, healthy, fulfilling relationship that you desire and deserve.

## SHE'S FRUSTRATED! HE THINKS SHE'S DIFFICULT!

When a woman doesn't know how to let a man know what's on her mind, she begins to show frustration. He interprets this as controlling. To her, she's holding resentment and frustrations on the inside to keep peace. Even though she thinks she's holding it all in, it seeps out and makes him feel like she's hard to deal with.

Timing is everything. It's best to ask God to reveal a time to express yourself to your man. A man equates a woman's frustration with her being a nag. When she goes off on him she makes him feel underappreciated and he says, "After all I've done for you, this is how you pay me back—unloved, uncared for?"

The man thinks, "I could have had relations with a woman who understands me and begs to be with me." He feels that he needs to step out with other women because he's doing all he can. He feels that if he's going to catch hell anyway he might as well catch hell for doing wrong. A woman should take the time to find a way that she can do things that will give her better results.

## CAN A CONFIDANT MAKE A GOOD PARTNER?

Sometimes a relationship can develop between friends who had no intentions of getting involved with each other. As they confide in each other and get closer the attraction grows and before you know it they have become lovers.

A woman should be sure the man she confides in has the qualities she seeks. Because she's not living with him every day she won't know what his package consists of. She should decide if she's willing to accept his likes, dislikes, and any other baggage that comes with him.

Any woman can put up with a man when she doesn't have to be with him every day. A woman should consider spending at least ninety days in a relationship with her confidant before she considers letting him be her permanent man.

## HE'S GOING TO BE HEAD OF THE HOUSEHOLD

The woman is sitting here miserable as hell. If she's going to marry a man she needs to check out more than just how fine he is. The woman has to realize that this man is going to be the head of her household and so if they decide to stay together she shouldn't settle for just anybody.

This also means that she's going to have to listen to him and work with him. He's probably going to have the last word in what happens and if he's an ignorant man she won't be ready for him.

## BE PREPARED TO MEET ELIGIBLE MEN

When a woman leaves her house, she should be presentable. When a woman least expects it, the man who's interested in her will show up. She should always be prepared to meet an eligible and available man when she's out running errands.

A woman thinks that because she's only running a short errand she can go out of the house looking any kind of way. Once she goes out she is caught off guard and the man she's interested in spots her looking ungroomed and crazy.

A woman should try to spend valuable time on her self-image before she even thinks of walking out the door. The effort she spends on her looks means a lot to an interested man. He can see that she cares and is motivated to take care of her. He becomes more interested in pursuing her when she looks good to him.

## LET SOMEONE KNOW YOUR PLANS

If the woman is sneaking around and trying to meet a new man or going out on a first date, she should be sure to let someone know. She should tell a best friend, cousin, daughter, son, or someone else.

Leave a note or a message on several people's voice mail. There are plenty of missing women who can't be found because they didn't leave a message.

## BE MINDFUL OF WHO'S GIVING COMPLIMENTS

When you walk into a room and guys are sitting around talking about parts of a woman's body, it's a turnoff, but to some women it's a turn-on.

A woman should be mindful of who's saying it. It might be someone desperate who will date anyone and is giving an empty compliment to get attention he does not deserve. Or it might be a gentleman who's giving her a worthy compliment. Be very careful about the compliments you receive because they are meant to bring you into his element, and the goal is hopefully to lead to sex.

## GET OVER IT

If a man hurts a woman's feelings she gets two or three days to drown in her own sorrow. Then she needs to get over it and move on. The longest walk in the world starts with just one step.

## DON'T PASS UP GOOD MEN

There are many women who wait around and pass up good men who God blessed them with. They think he's not fine enough or he's not a musclebound or he's too short or whatever. When a man wants a woman he finds a way to look past her flaws and many of her weaknesses. Women can't seem to do that.

A man can find a woman working in McDonald's with the little hat on and take her and make her his wife, but if he worked in Mc-Donald's she wouldn't look at him twice. Lessons come in all sizes and packages. Recognize a blessing when you receive it.

## SOMETIMES YOU'RE AHEAD AND DON'T EVEN REALIZE IT

The young woman who rides around with the guy who sells crack is living on borrowed time. He has the cars, suits, and diamonds, but none of that will mean anything when she ends up in jail just like him.

The girl who's making her living the right way can pass this woman just by working at McDonald's. The girl who's doing it the wrong way will eventually get caught and the girl who's living right will pass up everything she's doing.

The woman who's doing wrong will barely get phone calls and letters, but the woman who's doing right will have her freedom and be able to buy everything she wants. She'll really be ahead.

A woman should keep her word if she promises something will happen.

# Ten

# MARRIAGE

*Some women are so desperate to have a man that they will mess with a married man.*

Some people who are married don't know what the phrase "for better or worse" means. They expect marriage to be a lifelong fairy-tale romance. Sometimes everything is going good and then all of a sudden the "worse" kicks in for a few months.

Maybe she has picked him for his money and then the man gets sick. Now she's stuck with nursing him back to wellness or she's stuck with an invalid. She doesn't know what to do, but she was having fun when she was spending all his money. She's suffering just as much as he is. If only she had gotten married for the right reasons in the beginning. Anytime a woman does something for the wrong reasons she gets the wrong things in return.

## MARRYING A NOTHING MAN

Ladies, when you marry a "nothing man," don't ride the streets and tell everyone he's nothing. Try to fix it, get rid of him, or shut up.

The average woman starts breaking the man down when she

finds out he's a nothing man. Sometimes that's why a man can't be anything. The one person he trusts to build him up is the main person tearing him down. Talking bad about him and his shortcomings isn't treating him right. That makes a man feel like he's less than nothing.

Be a little more considerate about him and quit making it all about you. Give praise to him about how good he does things and say things like, "Ahh, that was nice." It makes a man feel stronger and he'll want to do more things for you. Men have very big egos and love when their woman strokes it. We are like puppies—we need to be stroked. It makes us want to do more for you.

There's the old saying, "You got to crawl before you walk." Things happen in life when you might have to be on a crutch or you might have to limp a little bit, but you don't necessarily have to crawl. The only time a woman should be on her knees is when she prays to the almighty God. Other than that, keep your butt off your knees. In your everyday life, quit crawling; just get up and walk.

## THE FAITHFUL MODE

I enjoy being faithful to my wife. I like watching what other women do when I'm trying to act right. They try to get me out of my faithful mode. They think they can get me to fall prey to them and that would make them look like a tough hottie.

## BEING A GOOD HUSBAND AND A GOOD MAN

Before a man can be a good man he has to get rid of all his childish ways and childish things. Things like chasing women, partying every night, and beating women must be put away. Before a man can be a God-fearing man he needs to turn his life around and put God first.

## A WOMAN SHOULD TAKE MARRIED MEN OFF HER LISTS

Let's face it, if a man is on his way out the door, leaving his family, and has a lot to offer, he still has baggage. If he's married to the woman he's leaving he has baggage that the new woman is usually not prepared for. Once he gets her he might do the same things to her that he did to his wife. Besides, a woman should never trust a man who leaves his wife for her. If he did it to the first one he might do it again.

If she must have this man she should make sure he has ended all intimate connections with his ex-wife before she starts an affair with him. She should allow him to become free before she even considers a relationship with him.

## HAVING AN AFFAIR WITH MARRIED MEN (CHRISTMAS)

I heard an old song, "What Do the Lonely Do for Christmas?" That's usually the question when a woman is messing with a married man or someone else's man. What does she do during the holidays?

A lot of times there's nothing she can do because she's sitting all alone. She soon realizes the man has other obligations. Now the holidays have arrived and she's waiting to get her presents. Oh, she can get her presents before or after the holidays, but she probably won't get them on Christmas.

Most men will be with their family so he has to lie to his wife and say he's going to the store so he can sneak and see the mistress for a few minutes.

The mistress is just a pastime. And it's a doggone shame that the woman would put herself in a position to become that.

## MARRIED MEN AND DESPERATE WOMEN

Some women are so desperate that they will mess with a married man. That's the wrong road to go down. Such a woman thinks she's getting a man, but what she's getting is an evil spirit. She's putting that evil spirit inside of her every time she has sex with him. Once the man gets inside of her he goes his way. The woman then meets another man, but she hasn't got rid of the last evil spirit yet.

Even though she still has the last man's spirit inside of her, she brings another man in her life and his spirit is inside of her too. Now her life is going bad and it's a total wreck and she can't seem to figure it out. A woman should start looking at her life situations. There's no rule that she can't have a man, but she often goes wrong because her insides are calling for a man. If she works on herself and allows God to work, she will not believe the good man He sends her. She needs to let the idea of having a man rest for a while and get men out of her system. She should cleanse her system and watch whom God sends to her.

A woman should never trust a man who leaves his wife for her.

# Eleven

# My Wives

*To get something that you never had you have to do something that you never did.*

People should try something different if what they are doing doesn't work. My current wife is more corporate. She's quiet and more of a refined woman. She's a grown woman. I knew when I began dating her that I would have to change some things about me. She made me want to change.

We were friends for about five years and I got married during those years to another young lady. Of course she was happy for me, but she was also a little hurt because she thought she had lost a friend. She still remained my friend and she was there for me when I was going through my divorce. Before I got my divorce she tried to talk me into going to counseling and getting help, but I knew that marriage was finished. I knew I had married the wrong woman because I did it for all the wrong reasons.

While I was going through the divorce I had hell in me and I was trying to control my wife at the time. I wasn't going to let this woman do me bad or treat me any kind of way in my own house. It could have easily been a physical fight, since I had hit women in the past. I guess I thought hitting women was what worked because I saw my father do it. But one of the things I promised God when I was changing myself was I would never hit another woman. So, to keep from hitting this woman, my current wife who was my friend at the time would say, "Why don't you come over here to stay?" Since no one slept upstairs in her house I would stay upstairs. It was a friendly arrangement. She would come get my clothes when I needed them cleaned or washed and she always asked me if I needed anything to eat. She took care of me and never asked for anything in return. I would watch her actions and say to myself, "Man, this is a good woman."

What turned me on the most about my present wife was her quality. I thought I was still looking for the whore-type woman, and after all of that and her trying to make me act right with my former wife, she really realized that I was going through changes with the divorce. She agreed it would be best for me to move out before I ended up in jail, so she tried to help me as long as she could by trying to get my mind back right.

Ever since the moment I met my current wife I wanted to find her someone better than me—someone who was good enough for her. I recognized that she was a good woman, but not one time did I ever recognize that I would be good enough for her.

The Holy Spirit revealed it to me that no man on earth is good enough for this woman—so why don't you be that man. After my divorce was final I decided that we would date twice a week and she agreed. Two weeks turned into three and three turned into four and so forth until I asked her, "Will you marry me?"

She had nine sisters and three brothers who drilled me, and I passed the test. This was the first time I ever had to ask a woman's dad for her hand in marriage. This let me know that God was with me because I was doing something I had never done. My previous wife was someone I could live with, but now I'm married to someone I can't live without.

My wife is pretty good when it comes to handling herself. She knows how to put people in their place. She can say a few kind words to put *me* back in place when I start leaning back toward the person I used to be. When I start raising hell all she has to say is, "Boom, God hears you." What do I say after that . . . really? What could any man say? You know you've got to be careful with your statements. Now, if you're really married to a fool, and he says something after that in the wrong way, you don't have to be worried about him. You won't be married to him long because he won't exist. God will take him away.

So when she says things like that I get quiet, go in the other room, and be mad for a couple of hours, because I can't say anything back. I don't want to loosen my tongue so I contain myself, put myself in another frame of mind, and after thinking about it, patch things up with my wife. The angle my wife uses is a pretty smart one.

## WAITING ON A GENTLEMAN

When I first met my wife and we went into a building, she would stand by the door and wait. She would not go through the door until I opened it for her. At first, I would start laughing and say, "You're tripping, because that's not what I do." Then I would say to myself, "If this is part of her and I'm thinking about marrying her, I've got to give her the things she wants." Now I have no problem with it.

She's raising our daughter the same way. My daughter stands her little self by the door waiting on me to open it before she makes a move. That's so funny to me, the requirements real women have.

I'm cool with it, though, because it's proved the difference between a woman and a girl.

## I Used to Party Every Day

I used to go out and party seven days a week just to trap women. When I met my wife we became good friends. She wanted to take it deeper and I was kind of messing around, but then I started falling in love with her kindness. I slowly fell in love with the whole picture and everything she was doing.

She did things that made me pay attention. We weren't staying together or anything like that, but we were kind of dating and I told her, "I tell you what, we'll try this out. I'll spend time with you two days a week: Mondays and Sundays." Those were the days I wasn't doing a doggone thing. She said, "Okay, cool."

Most women would have gone crazy at the mention of me giving them a couple of days. They would have said, "You either spend time with me when I want or don't spend time with me at all." But she said, "That's fine with me."

So I started spending Mondays and Sundays with her. Then I started calling her on days I would leave the club and I found myself going by her place. She would unlock the door for me, and then I started spending Mondays, Tuesdays, and Wednesday with her. The next thing you know it was seven days a week and I was happy about it.

## It's Difficult to Have a Wife and Another Woman

I was with my first wife for about nine years and got married to her in the last two years of our relationship. I actually quit six women, and then two days later I got married.

Of course that didn't work because three months later I had all

six of them back, plus my wife. It's hard starting out into a relationship with a wife and a few women on the side. I found out that it
wouldn't work.

## THE FIRST LADY—THE LAST LADY

Every man, whether he's a preacher, policeman, or whoever, calls
his wife the first lady. I refuse to call my wife the first lady because
my mother was the first lady—the first lady I ever knew, the first
lady who ever took care of me. And calling my wife the first lady
always made me feel as if I had someone else coming. So, I decided
to call my wife the last lady because in my mind when I say last, I
know that's the end of it. I know this is the last woman I will ever
need. A wife is supposed to be the last lady a man wants to see, the
last lady in his life.

## LOVING MY WIFE

I got rid of one vice and went out and grabbed another vice, and
that is loving my wife. When she was my fiancé, she had a cold
move on me. I don't know if she was trying to do it, but she was
cold at it. She wanted me, so I figured why am I trying to convince a
woman to like me and understand who I am when I have someone
who wants me? All I needed to do is want her. So what I did is go
beyond her wants and want her more than she wanted me.

## MAKING LOVE WITH YOUR BEST FRIEND

You'd better be careful when you have sex with your best friend.
That's a dangerous situation because it can go either way. I tried it
several times and it never worked for me. After you have sex with
your friend you start feeling guilty or kind of funny about it. It always feels like something is wrong although I'm pretty sure there

are some exceptions to that rule and it works for some people, but it never worked for me.

## My Wife Is Beautiful on the Inside

Another beautiful thing I like about my wife is she won't go to bed mad. My wife tries to hold up to that. I'll go to bed mad for a month with my mouth stuck out like I'm just some crazy fool. I get mad over little stuff, and that's just the way I am. But my wife won't do that.

Before she goes to bed she'll say "I love you" and "I'm sorry." Even if it wasn't her fault she'll say she's sorry. And if she goes to sleep while waiting on me to get home she'll wake up the next morning and clear things up.

But me, I'm still mad all night and the next day. I'm a fool. I'm the kind of guy who will step on a person's foot and wait on the person whose foot I stepped on to say they're sorry. Just know, God is still working on parts of me. I can be real crazy at times.

## What Made Me Marry My Wife?

It was a number of things, but I can truly say I got serious about her when I quit sharing what I had with the world and just started directing everything I had into one place. Love grew from me, giving everything I had to one person instead of two or three.

Whatever you share, share it in one place, and then something else will take over and make everything wonderful. I know that you can still get fooled no matter how saved you are or how you're trying to help yourself or stay away from another person. You can still be attracted to another person. I asked my wife to keep her hair the same way and just stay the same. If she comes out of the room looking different, then I won't feel like I'm attracted to a different type woman. Now I can handle her changes.

## JUST STAND

It's a wonderful thing being married. It has its good days and bad days, but I want to ask the fellows a question: "While you're dating three and four women, have all the days been good or do you have bad days too?"

I'd rather have a woman who understands. If I don't have but five dollars in my pocket we can still do something and be happy with it. I don't care if it's simply going down the street and buying two honey buns. At least we'll be fighting this battle together.

Five dollars is a lot of money for two people in love. Of course if a women considers a man a loser because all he has is five dollars, then he might want to reconsider who she is and what she's about. He might want to ask, "Is this the woman I need in my life?"

As the Bible says, "Just stand." You'll be surprised what can happen for a woman if she just stands.

## HUMPTY DUMPTY HAD A GREAT FALL

What keeps me from messing around on my wife is that I don't ever want to break her heart. I don't want to lose that 150 percent that she gives me. A man doesn't understand that when he has a woman who gives her all, he should recognize that she could change on him. Once he hurts her and breaks her heart she'll only give him 40 to 50 percent. Oh, she'll still love him, she'll still be with him, and she'll even stick by him, but he better believe that she's torn apart on the inside. Put it this way: he still can't put Humpty Dumpty together again. Once a man shatters a woman's heart it's hard to put all the pieces back together.

Do as you would do when someone is trying to fight you and your daddy is standing there to protect you—stand tall.

# Twelve

# FAMILY

*What a person does, will have to be paid back later.*

I used to get mad at the relationship my wife had with her father. I guess I was jealous. She would always say, "I miss my dad. I want to go home and see my dad." I would say, "Girl, get over here. You got a new family now." Now that I've gotten comfortable with my wife she can her love her dad all she wants, but now I want her to love me as much as she loves her dad.

I ask myself, "If she's giving her dad all that love, then what in the world does she have for me?" I'm just going to lie back and see what kind of love she has for me and quit trying to stop her from loving someone else. I never knew about fatherly love because my father was never around.

I was around my kids when they were young, but something happened along the way and I got thrown off the trail. I got a divorce and had to leave the home and now my kids probably don't know fatherly love either. I thank God for putting another child in my life so I can experience what fatherly love is and reach back to my kids.

## THINGS YOU DO CAN COME BACK ON YOU

Before I was born a man died and took up for me. The least I can do before I die is take a stand and take up for him. Out of all the stuff I've been through I now know why people say, "What a person does they'll have to pay back later." That's what happened to me.

Everything I've done wrong, I ended up paying back. I've had bad luck and misfortune because of all I've done to people. It's kind of like a skunk when the wind changes direction: he says, "It's all coming back to me now." After using everybody I've smelled my own behind too.

The truth will set you free. I believe it because when I told women the whole truth, they let me go.

# Thirteen

# CHILDREN

*God bless the child that's got his own.*

When I was a growing up I kept watching guys who had everything and the girls wanted them. Every woman knows another woman who's young and ahead of her financially, and she thinks, *Wow,* I want to be just like her.

Well, they say the early bird gets the worm, but what worm are we really talking about? It's like going to school and the head cheerleader or the quarterback of the football team or the most popular person in the school—everybody seems to care about him or her.

Some of these same kids are the people who ended up being on crack, got abused, or became alcoholics because the fame game happened too soon for them.

If more people would wait for their turn to come around, everything would be okay. Don't worry about the person who's in front of you right now because you can easily pass her.

## If a Younger Person Decides to Read This Book

This section is for the young girls twenty to twenty-five years old who think they want to date older men.

If a woman is in her twenties and she's dating a man who's at least fifteen years older, how does she expect him to treat her like a lady when she isn't even a grown woman yet? Most twenty-year-olds don't even know what it takes to be grown because they haven't gone through enough yet.

As soon as a man treats her like a kid, she gets mad and starts looking at him crazily and says, "Hey, don't treat me like a kid!" Well, I'm sorry to tell her that that's what she's acting like. She should try to find a man no more than five years older than she is when she's that young. If the man is fifteen years older that's bad, but when she gets in her thirties and forties, maybe she can deal with the age difference. By then she's lived and has had a chance to experience some things in life.

She should quit wasting her youth on old men and first gain those experiences. She should get with somebody her age and then she can learn how to love and care for people in her age bracket. Once she's learned a few more things about life and love, then she can jump back over where the old men are.

## Boys and Girls Are Trying to Be Men and Women Too Soon

There's a new game where young boys and girls try to be men and women before their time. They are so confused because they don't know how to reach real manhood and womanhood yet.

It takes a lifetime to learn how to be a man and a woman. They're doing young stuff, which later turns out to be old stuff. It's the same old games that people play. It's really no new games out there. Oh, they can put a new tweak here and there, but it's really the same old game. So, young people don't go around saying, "Oh, he's old, they don't even do that no more."

"Oh, yes they do and a kid doesn't even know it until after their behind is done doing it." I suggest young boys and girls quit worrying about what people don't do anymore and start worrying about what they *shouldn't* do anymore.

## CHILD SUPPORT

Let's discuss this child support thing. I know at some time or another every woman needs help, but ladies, let's be fair about this. Just because a man is making extra money and the woman is no longer a part of his life, doesn't mean she has to seek revenge or be angry with him.

The woman should stop trying to be greedy and get more from the man. It's so much better if there's peace in the relationship because she might be able to get her child extra money. But she could also give her child extra problems by trying to get the extra money.

The child sees the changes her mom and dad are going through when they fuss and fight. The child knows that his daddy is not coming back because if he does it's going to be some mess with the mother. If the woman just goes about her business, God will make a way for her and He's going to make sure the guy that's making the extra money pays. Something is going to happen to him in his life where he's going to need that child one day. So, the woman should quit trying to beat the man up for the child and let life beat his butt. This is bigger than the woman. It's already handled. It's already written, so she can lay down somewhere, stop worrying, and rest her mind.

## THINK ABOUT THE CHILDREN

When a woman says she wants to leave she probably hasn't thought about her children. Okay, what about them? If a woman is single and has children she should have thought of them when she met the man.

When she brought the man into her home she wasn't even thinking about her children. All she thought about when she tried to get the man was her womanly wants and needs.

## WAITING UNTIL THE CHILDREN GROW UP

When a woman decides to wait until the children grow up before she leaves, the man knows that it's not about the kids. It's all about the woman feeling it's too much trouble to get out there and find someone new.

A woman will say that she doesn't want to leave because of the children, but in reality she's staying because she wants to be there. The children are not the reason she's staying or leaving.

## WOMEN WHO INTRODUCE MEN TO THEIR CHILDREN TOO SOON

A woman who brings a man into her children's lives too soon is headed in the wrong direction. A woman should not give any man that privilege with her children.

There should be a waiting period before a new man meets the children. Why not bring God into their lives? The woman should be sure to date the man for a while before her children ever see him in their home. The woman is taking her home and her children for granted when men are presented to her children before the waiting period is up.

A woman should openly talk with her children and prepare them when she's thinking about having a relationship with a new man.

## THE WOMAN'S CHILDREN SHOULD LOOK GOOD TOO

A woman should remember, if she's going to look good, her children should also look good. Her children are a reflection of her. She looks fraudulent if she looks good and her children don't.

A man will look down on a woman who allows her children to look bad. In a man's eyes the woman is a perpetrator, a fake, even unfit.

A real woman is going to take care of her kids no matter what it takes. Her children's lives should be in order from feeding them to clothing them properly. It's a total package. She should have pride about herself and her children. If she doesn't have much money at least she can work to do things to improve her life. If she has something going on at least the man will think she's making strides.

## THE HUNT FOR A MAN TAKES CONTROL
## OF SOME WOMEN

When a woman is trying to find a man she doesn't have time to watch her kids anymore. She's on a manhunt because she's trying to find another daddy. She does this because she's lonely. Now her son is alone and sitting inside her house writing rap songs with bad lyrics saying that women are animals, and he's doing this in her house. She doesn't know because once again she's out there trying to find her kids another daddy and herself another lover.

When a woman is out in the dating world she should remember to prioritize involvement with her children.

## CHILDREN AND MUSIC

Women want the record labels to stop producing offensive kinds of CDs, but the record labels don't want their creators to stop because they're making money. If a mother really wants it to stop, she has to go in there and look in her child's bedroom and look at that piece of paper or look at the CD he's burning off his laptop. He might even play it for her and when she hears it she thinks to herself, "That boy sure got talent." What she's really saying is he can rap and she hasn't heard a word in the song.

## MOTHERS, PAY ATTENTION TO YOUR DAUGHTERS

Women need to stop worrying about men so much and start paying attention to their daughters. Teach them how to be independent young ladies and get close enough to ask them personal questions.

So many times a woman will have a boyfriend who's looking at her daughters in the wrong way and something can be happening behind her back and she never notices it. She's so busy worrying about her little relationship that she doesn't pay attention to what's going on before her own eyes.

And even if her daughter tells her about it she won't believe it. She doesn't want to think the man is that way. The daughter will tell her mother that the man looked at her a certain way and he said inappropriate things and her mom won't pay attention to it. Because she wants a relationship so bad she'll sacrifice her children for this man. That's very wrong. Women need to pay closer attention!

## MY OLDEST DAUGHTER AND ME

My relationship with my oldest daughter is not where I would like it to be at this time, but I realized that I have to let her come around when she wants to. I wasn't there for her physically when she was growing up.

Women should teach their children to capture the moments they have left and just because the man wasn't there in the beginning doesn't mean he doesn't want to be there now. Girls need their daddies no matter how old they are.

One day, hopefully she'll understand that my arms are open, I'll always be there for her, and I love her very much.

## FATHERS RAISING THEIR DAUGHTERS

I want to touch on fathers raising their daughters, leading them in the right direction but feeling like they themselves are failures. Here's the problem as I see it. As a dad, I can tell my daughter what not to do because this is going to happen or that will happen. But the guy in the street won't tell her what not to do. He's going to try and talk her into doing all the things he wants her to do and only some of what she wants to do.

After a woman hears what she shouldn't do and what she can't do, her want-to-dos override all her teachings of what not to do. It's like losing weight. She knows what not to eat, but when someone tells her not to eat it, she wants it more than ever. Her mind makes her do exactly what she's not supposed to do.

## WOMEN RESPECT MEN WHO TAKE CARE
## OF THEIR CHILDREN

Men often have children from a previous marriage; something happened to the wife or maybe she ran off and left her family. If he's taking care of his children he can find a woman faster than a single man. It's because the woman knows the man who's taking care of his children is responsible. Guys don't understand that.

She'll find men who deny they have children, and then she'll find out he has ten of them. Or he'll proudly say he's got five kids and the woman will find out later that he's not taking care of them. His child support is so far behind that he's on the run from the government. So I understand how women respect a man who's taking care of his children. They're saying, "At least he's responsible. If he's taking care of his kids from a previous relationship and she's gone, he must not be a bad guy.

## MY CHILDREN
My wife, my stepdaughter, and I went over to my ex-wife's house. My stepdaughter is a young lady full of love and hugs me a lot. She just loves her new dad.

Once my other daughter saw the displays of affection, she thought I was leaving her out, but it wasn't that. I missed being in her life. I was a foolish man during that period of my life and I didn't know the importance of having a father-daughter relationship. I see that I hurt her because I didn't spend quality time with her. My relationship with my oldest daughter is something I work at every day. It's not where I want it to be, but I pray one day it will be.

If a woman decides to let a man go, that's fine, but allow him the opportunity to spend time with his children. A father-and-child relationship is so important to the character of the child. Let him love his children and quit telling his kids he's not this or he's not that. The children are going to find out who he is in the long run . . . anyway.

## BE CAREFUL WHAT YOU DO AROUND YOUR DAUGHTER
Ladies, be careful what you do around your daughter because she learns everything from you. If your daughter learns from you and you're in her face acting whorish, chances are she's going to act that way.

I'm a changed man. I want to help people who are down and out and bring them back to where they know there's a God.

# Fourteen

# FRIENDS

*Asking your friends for advice concerning your man can ruin a potentially great relationship.*

Quit letting your girlfriend, your mama, or your brother pick the man they think should be in your life. A woman should remember that the relatives are going to go home and she'll be left with a fool she didn't want in the first place. Don't choose him because somebody else thought it was a good idea.

A woman should understand that the people who picked the man for her won't have to deal with him on a daily basis. She should pick her own man with her own heart and her own emotions.

## OLD MEMORIES DO NOT MEAN GOOD TIMES

A woman often gets that little itch in her panties after her girlfriends have told her how good their man was in bed. Now she's saying things like, "Last night, girrrrl, ooooooh I had the time of my life with my man." A woman who doesn't have a man feels that she needs to be able to respond by doing or saying something just as spectacular. It causes her to start reminiscing about the great feelings she had with her old relations. She then starts to play games with her own mind and is tempted to go back and call men from her past.

## WATCH OUT FOR YOUR GIRLFRIENDS
A woman loves to tell her girlfriends about how she cussed her man out and how no man is going to run over her. She's trying to be tough, but she knows she's weak as a lamb when it comes to that man.

But her girlfriends don't know she still wants him and they might believe that she's really through with the man, so now the girlfriends are looking at him and believe it's really over. They think the man is free to be pursued. Now the girlfriends feel they can get him.

## WOMEN WHO FALL FOR SIMPLE THINGS
I know how to create a paper rose out of a bar napkin and that would excite a woman. She would get so caught up in me that she would let her guard down. I have fooled many women by telling them what they want to hear. I would tell them:

- "Tell your mama I said thank you, because she did a beautiful job on you."
- "I'm *not* trying to be fresh; I'm just trying to be friendly."
- "God provided you with your needs; I'll provide you with your wants."

These lines worked on so many women that it even surprised me. They automatically put a woman in a comfort zone. I would make a woman believe I didn't want anything and then she would let me use my little catch lines on her.

Men use lines a lot, so a woman shouldn't fall prey to them.

## DON'T BE JEALOUS OF YOUR FRIEND'S HAPPINESS

A woman should not get jealous when she recognizes that her friend has a man. If she sees that they are doing well and getting their lives and families in order, she should try her best not to envy them.

She should always wish them well and support their success. Just because they are buying things and appearing to be content should not make her jealous.

If a woman and her man's relationship is not as cozy as her friend's, that's okay because time might have the answer. The friend might be going home, closing that door, and getting beat up by the same man you think is providing her happiness. She might be happy. Whatever the case, be happy for her if she's happy.

## IF A FRIEND SEES HER MAN CHEATING

If a woman spots her best friend's man having an affair she should not get involved. She should not mention or tell it. She should stay out of it. If she chooses to tell her friend about the affair she is risking the friendship and becoming involved in something that could get blown out of proportion.

The friend who is being cheated on will probably appreciate the information, but now she has to do something about it because she knows that others have witnessed it. Now she has to act a fool. She keeps it to herself when she doesn't think anyone else knows, and she probably already knew about it anyway.

Being told of the infidelity of her man will cause problems with a man who she really loves. Now the relationship is damaged. The woman who told it thought she was helping, when she was actually ruining a relationship that might have had a better chance because maybe they could work through it.

## Stop Getting Fooled by Your Girlfriends

A woman's girlfriends will be the first to say, "I don't like him. He's not this and he's not that," or they'll say, "You better watch him, he's no good."

Be careful of the person who always has something negative to say about your relationship or your man. She might be the very one trying to get him. Just go by what you like and don't let others' opinions affect yours. They're afraid you'll end up caring for him too much, and if you start spending a lot of time with him you won't see them as much and that might be why they don't like him, so check the girlfriends out first.

## Taking Advice from Women Who Don't Have a Man

A woman will run out and ask her single girlfriend what she thinks about this or that situation with her man. The girlfriend will tell her what she thinks, and as the woman begins to follow what her friend has to say the woman taking the advice goes wrong. The woman giving the advice probably doesn't have a man. Taking bad advice from this kind of friend is detrimental to the relationship.

If a woman decides to involve another person in her relationship problems, she should be prepared for the consequences.

## Keeping Good Friends

I have a friend who helps me a lot around my house. He knows me well and we used to build homes and remodel stuff together. He's always been there to talk to me. When he gets in a situation, he calls me and says, "Dawg, what you think about this?" And I'll tell him and he'll say, "That sounds good, you're right."

If he is dating a girl or something, he'll ask me what do I think and my suggestion to him is, "Stop looking for women with no self-value and start looking for a woman with wife qualities." He agrees with me. We've been friends for maybe ten or fifteen years. And we're still pretty tight.

There's another friend I'm very close to. We have a working relationship and a friendship. He doesn't see the changes in me because he's too close to me. When a person works around someone all day long they don't really see the changes that everyone else sees. Being around a person every now and then gives them a better vision of the changes being made in a person's appearance. It's kind of like seeing yourself. You don't see yourself changing, but you might see somebody who you haven't seen in five or six years. They might think things like, "Wow, she's having a hard time" or "Wow, she's really looking good." They might even make remarks like, "You've lost weight" or "You're taking care of yourself."

And that's the way it is when a woman is around her man every day. He doesn't really see the change in her, but others do. Other people will say, "That sister has really changed."

My wife is always asking, "How do you keep so many friends?" I talk to people I've been friends with for thirty years who still call me and keep up with me.

There's something good about a person when people are still calling and keeping in touch. That shows there's something about this person that people like. Some people don't have one friend, or anyone at all calling them, because they're doing something wrong in their life to people. Watch a man and his friendships; this tells a woman a lot about him.

## WHAT IS YOUR CHARACTER

I was always a little crazy. One day I talked to a celebrity director friend of mine and he brought something out when I was talking to him. He said, "You just couldn't come out of your character."

I never looked at it as my character. I looked at it as real life, and something I made myself into. When he said it, it rung a bell. It struck something within me that said "*Wow*, that *was* my character!" I appreciate him for saying it. If I had never talked to him about this, then I would have never gotten this valuable information. Some men are good men; they just haven't come out of their bad character.

## YOUNG IS GOOD, BUT OLDER IS BETTER

When a woman is young she doesn't necessarily know men who are good in ways that an older woman would. When a woman gets older she looks for men with qualities that have more substance.

A young woman may look for a man who's fine, but an older woman wants a man with bragging rights. Make sure your bragging rights are more than his looks. A woman should look for the kind of man she feels can make her glad to be alive. It's acceptable to be a young fool, but there's no fool like an old fool. Being a young and dumb man has no place in an older and wiser woman's world.

## REAL FRIENDSHIPS LAST

They say, "If a man can find a friend, one friend in his whole entire life, he's found a pot of gold." I can say honestly I've got three best friends. My main guy friend lives in Tulsa, Oklahoma.

I grew up with him and went to school with him. We both got married around the same time. Later we were staying in the same neighborhood and didn't know it. We hosted fashion shows together. We got married a second time and moved to the same neighborhood again.

He's the only guy who knew me well enough for me to call and tell him when I'd done something. He would talk to me, but back then I was ignorant as hell. He would also call and talk to me when somebody was saying he was acting crazy. We're still friends and we're about the same age. We've shared over forty years of friendship. He's my main friend and I still respect him and he respects me, and we have love for each other. Right now, I can still call him and tell him that he needs to talk to his boy.

My wife calls him when I'm trouble and his wife calls me when he's trouble. I guess that will keep going on until one of us passes. We never take it too far or get in heated arguments because it's not good for two fools to be mad at each other.

When he hears me talk now and I tell him where I'm headed or where I'm going with my life, he's proud of it, but he doesn't believe it because he never knew anyone could be as far left as I was and come back right. He's constantly saying, "I don't believe this, but I am proud of you."

I trust his judgment that I am changing and I know everything is going to be all right with God and me.

## A GOOD FRIEND IS LIKE A GOOD WOMAN OR MAN

If a woman can find one true friend, that's a beautiful thing, but I always hear women say, "She befriended me." A friend is like a good woman or a good man. They're hard to find.

### IF YOU KNOW GOD, WHY ARE YOU DOING WRONG?

I also hear many women say, "I'm going to be fine because I know God." Many times a woman is doing everything she wants to do when she knows that it's not right.

If I were the woman I would be afraid because *I* do know God. Keep on and see what happens if you keep doing wrong.

Quit letting your girlfriend, your mama, or your brother pick the man they think should be in your life.

# Fifteen

# DATING

*It's very difficult for a man to spend his money and time on a woman if he's not getting anything out of the deal.*

*After a woman has been with the man a few times she starts prioritizing sex just the same as the man does.*

If a man asks you to go out of town with him and you say, "Yes," he's going to get one room. Don't even think that he's going to get two rooms and don't even suggest it. Stay at home if you can't deal with being in one room with your travel partner.

If a woman feels that she should have her own room and he doesn't want to get the room, she should either pay to get a separate room or stay at home. Don't stay in his room if you don't want to. You're not obligated just because you're out of town with him. Getting an invitation to an out-of-town date means one thing to a man: "Let's get away and things are going to go my way."

It's very difficult for a man to spend his money and time on a woman if he's not getting anything out of the deal. He feels it's wasting his time, money, and effort. That's the way men see it. Men and women don't always see things the same way. She sees oranges; he sees apples. Same category, but different things.

## QUIT DATING THE REPRESENTATIVE

Stop dating the person who the man is representing and date the person behind the representative. Understand that when a woman meets a man in the store or the park, she should know he's just a representative. Know who the man is behind the mask. What he's showing to the woman is only a representative.

## COURTSHIP!

What does court mean? It's a place where you bring a person in front of the jury for questioning of their credibility. The jury is your friends and family who will keep a sharp eye on the potential mate. This process will let you know if he's ready for the ship.

- *Ship.* When you say ship you think of a journey.
- *Courtship.* A time for presenting the facts to take on a journey. Courtship is more important than bullship.

So you got to go through the courtship to see if this person is qualified enough to go on the journey with you.

## INTERNET DATING

Internet dating presents a seemingly endless supply of possible dates. And there's no way to check to keep people honest. A significant fraction of Internet daters behave quite rudely. For example, people have experienced:

- Potential dates setting plans to meet, but never showing up or apologizing.
- Potential dates announcing an intention to meet, and then ignoring any follow-up about plans.
- Potential dates ignoring e-mails sent to them or even responses to their initial e-mails.

Much of this behavior is rude, and there's little explanation other than lack of decency. After all, it's much easier to cordially say no by e-mail than to do it by phone.

So here are some rules—developed after discussion with other Internet daters—regarding what situations deserve a response.

## AFTER THE FIRST CONTACT

If someone contacts you, you don't have to respond. Some dating sites do ask you to send a "decline contact" autoreply. I think a response—whether simply an autoreply or a brief note—is appropriate if the approach is sincere and the person is reasonably in your ballpark.

However, if the person who contacts you sends a form letter, or is clearly outside your stated parameters (age, geography, etc.), then a reply isn't necessary.

It's always good to stress the unpredictability of chemistry, rather than your analysis of the person's faults. So write, "Thanks for your note, but I don't think we're a match," rather than, "Thanks for your note, but you're way too fat/bald/poor/materialistic for me."

## IF YOU CHANGE YOUR MIND BEFORE MEETING

It's possible that you might have exchanged an e-mail or two—even a phone call—but you have changed your mind about meeting. Maybe you've learned some more about them and realize the potential has diminished. Or maybe you've met a better match.

Here you obviously have to be more careful, because earlier in the sequence you did entertain the possibility that a match was possible. Try something like, "I'm sorry, but I now think we're not as good a match as I hoped, so I'll wish you luck."

## AFTER A MEETING

It's okay, after one date or even two, to simply let things lapse. Mutual silence speaks for itself. However, if one of you does follow up, it's rude to just ignore it. It's better to simply say something like, "I'm glad we made the effort to meet, but I don't think we're a match."

What if someone violates these rules? Yes, it's tempting to upbraid them. But they've already moved on, so why waste your energy on someone who clearly isn't right for you? Try to focus on the next person, and assume the best, until proven otherwise.

Bad Internet manners feed on themselves. Once you've been treated rudely, you might think it's okay to treat the next person badly. Don't let that happen. A little courtesy goes a long way. And karma is a boomerang.

## COMPUTER LOVE

I don't understand computer love. If you can't find a man in real life and you look for love on the Internet, be careful. That might be a way of getting to know the person from the inside out.

Keep in mind that there are exceptions to every rule. You also might find a murderer, a rapist, or just a good lonely man, but that's a tough one right there.

People say if you just talk to God like you talk to your best friend He'll answer you. All I know is what He told me right after I talked to Him. So I'm going to do this thing in the name of Jesus.

# Sixteen

# GOD GIVES US CHOICES

*If you give somebody something and just be quiet about it, watch what God gives you in return!*

I think the greatest thing God gives man is choice. We all have the opportunity to make good choices, but we often fail to make them because we are scared of the outcome. Most women are scared of the unknown. When a woman gives, she should give from her heart and she shouldn't make the man feel guilty because he gave from a different place. If a woman gives from her heart, the person she gave it to shouldn't feel like he is obligated to her or owes her for doing it. Making a man feel guilty is trickery, instead of truly giving. The woman giving should never turn around and give with a rubber band attached to the gift so it can be pulled back and worked in a way to control a person's life. Just let it go! When a gift is given, never brag on what you gave. I was told that when you give to someone and you tell everybody, your blessing is the fact that you are able to tell that you gave. If you give somebody something and just be quiet about it, watch what God gives you in return!

## KNOW WHAT YOU WANT

One thing I loved about my wife when I was dating her is she knew what she wanted. Plenty of people tried to talk her out of dating me, but that wasn't what she wanted. She knew she had found her man and she knew what she wanted. *Me.* She had a beautiful daughter who would always hide from me. When she thought I saw her hiding, she would run and hug me. After a while her daughter started calling me dad, but of course she stopped her from doing that and told her to call me Mr. Boom. We didn't know if it was going to last. Her daughter told me one day, "I'll be glad when you and my mom get married." I asked her why and she said, "So I can call you daddy." I would visit my wife before we got married and eat dinner, laugh, talk, or hang out and we would spend quality time together. When my wife and I got married, the preacher said, "You may now kiss the bride," I kissed my wife and my little girl said "Daddy!" She ran down the aisle and hugged me. That was one of the greatest feelings I ever had in my life: Two women standing there and loving me, when I didn't even have one who I thought cared.

## STOP MAKING MEN FIGHT

Women have got to stop making men fight and making a man think she's worth fighting for. When a man does something wrong to her she should ask God to forgive him and she should forgive him too.

## WILL HE CATCH YOU IF YOU FALL

Sometimes a woman needs a man but knows that he's not there. And she falls for him anyway. Who in the world is going to catch her when she falls? She should make sure he's there before she falls for him because she might not get caught.

## NEVER TAKE NAKED PHOTOS OR MAKE VIDEOTAPES

When a woman gets caught in the moment and she feels excited, she should not be so weak that she allows naked photos to be taken. No matter how many times the man says he won't use the photos, he's lying. As soon as he gets angry or finds a way to make money with the photos he will show them to others.

## WHEN IS IT TIME TO LEAVE?

Many women wonder when it is best to leave a man, and when she will know she's had enough. To find the answer she should think about this old saying: "I'm not a doctor, but I know when my patience is getting short."

## DON'T *DO* A MAN WHO DOES DRUGS

If a woman dates a man and she finds out that he does drugs, she should stop the relationship right there. If he offers her a hit of cocaine or marijuana or whatever and he knows ahead of time that she doesn't do drugs, she should stop it before it starts. If he does drugs and she doesn't . . . really . . . how much further do you think this thing can go? If he really cares, he'll never try to get her to join him and he'll quit doing them. It's going to be a rough one because most of the time a woman's heart is so involved that the bad overrides the good. The woman is usually so green she doesn't know which way to go. She figures if the man allows her to do drugs with him, maybe he will like her more. So she starts liking the drugs more and the next thing you know she's asking him to stop by and pick up some before he comes over. Now she's hooked and he's ready to move on.

## DRUGS LEAD TO NOTHING POSITIVE

If you're dating a man and both of you do drugs, you're going to go nowhere together. You have to wonder, Are the drugs so important that she would need them just to settle for a man who's already nothing? What if she gets pregnant and has a baby? That means one thing, she still won't have anything. Now she has a baby who belongs to this nothing of a man and now she's surrendered to being nothing so she won't chance making him feel like less than a man. You have to find a man who's not just talking the talk, but also walking the walk. Your phrase for the day should be.

*Show me!*

## IN SO MUCH PAIN THAT YOU'RE ADDICTED

Are you doing drugs or alcohol because you're in pain? Has your man left you? Is he acting up? Are you confused and don't know what to do? If so, please get help. Go to counseling or find a mentor. Go back to your family to be reminded that you have one. They will help you remember your values, if you ever had some. Alcohol and drugs don't fix anything. They only make things worse and in the end you only hurt the ones you love.

## MOVING IN WITH A MAN

When a woman moves into a man's house without having her own, the man places her in a slave category. She leaves her mama or her cousin's house to move in with him, knowing that her mama was glad she left in the first place. If she doesn't play her cards right, she'll have to turn around and go back to her cousin's house. But her cousin doesn't want her back there because she wouldn't get off her behind and do anything for herself. She calls her girlfriends and tells them to come by and check it out and now she's busy showing all her friends and acquaintances how good she's living. Once she starts bragging on how she's living the man can pretty much treat her any kind of way because she doesn't want to be embarrassed or look like a failure.

## IF HE CHEATS, TAKE ACTION

As soon as a man decides to tell a woman the truth, she can't handle it. Many times guys will sweep stuff under the rug and just let it go because they don't have to make any decisions on it.

When the woman finds out the truth she feels that she has to make a decision: "Do I stay?" "Do I get help?" Many more questions of this nature have to be dealt with, but they open doors that the man doesn't want to deal with and the woman can't handle. A woman doesn't want to take herself through the necessary changes to fix it or heal from it. Even though actions speak louder than words, women avoid taking action. Women use their voices instead of their heads. They rant and rave, cuss and fuss, threaten to leave or threaten to be unfaithful, when all they really have to do is take action. Action creates results. Talking about what you're going to do won't fix the problem. A woman has to take some kind of action.

## HAVE A PLAN B

Ask yourself, what are you prepared to do? Are you prepared to go if you have to? Always have a Plan B (backup plan). Have somewhere to go just in case it doesn't work out as planned. The woman has to have somewhere to go when the man is messing up.

## GOD GIVES YOU WHAT YOU NEED IN TIME

One thing that I can relate to is that God gives each of us what He wants us to have when He's ready for us to have it. If He gives it to a woman before her time, she won't be able to keep it because she won't know what to do with it. I know because it has happened to me before. Faith without work is dead.

## RESCUE YOURSELF

A woman should learn to rescue herself and if the time comes when she has to do it again she'll already know how to survive. If she keeps leaning on everybody else to help her, she won't know how to do it for herself.

If she refuses to help herself, she might as well surrender and let the man do her any way he wants. It's her fault if he mistreats her because all it takes is a little bit more work to be something in life. If women quit looking for the easy way out, they will be better prepared for survival. Conquer the hard stuff and the easy things will come.

God didn't give any one person everything, but He did give something to everyone.

# Seventeen

# CHANGE

*Don't let a man touch you until you find the right man.*

*I'm a changed man. I want to experience what it feels like to touch people's hearts in a giving way.*

God made us all different. A woman will put unnecessary pressure on herself because she's trying to be somebody else. Be who you are, then try to be the best you can be. If you work to be who you truly are, you'll be in a comfort zone and not out of your element. Being a copycat wasn't your assignment when God placed you on earth.

## CHANGE FOR ME HAS BEEN GOOD
I have gone through changes in my life that have caused a change in me. There are things that happened to me that softened my heart. There was a time in my life when no one could tell me what to do because I didn't want people to think I was a punk who could be pushed around. I would go against myself to keep others from thinking they made me do something.

I watched Oprah give to others for three days and she brought joyful tears to my eyes and joy to my heart. To see the joy on people's faces when they received something made me think. I said, "Wow, I'm getting kind of weak." That made me say to myself, "I have to find a way to get rich so that I can experience what it feels like to touch people's hearts in that way." Right now, all I have is Christ so I'm hoping that Christ can make me rich and allow me to give instead of always receiving. I have never felt that feeling before, even though people have given me things in my life. Have you ever felt so joyful that you experienced a choked-up feeling from giving a person something? I want that feeling. I want to see what it feels like to give people hope when hope is gone. I want to help people who are down and out and bring them back to where they know there is a God.

## NEVER DEMAND SHE DO *ANYTHING* TO PROVE HER LOVE

A man should never make a woman do anything she doesn't already do. If he does he might find that she likes it. For example, asking her to be with another woman. Oh, I could have married a dyke and we could have chased women together, or invited girls over, but I was aware that she could have liked women more than she liked me and that would have been a problem because someone would have always been in our mix. When a wholesome woman takes her marriage vows and loves her man so much that she's willing to do *anything* for him, he should be careful of what he asks her to do.

## A MAN SHOULD NOT TRY TO FORCE A WOMAN TO CHANGE

If a woman doesn't party and her man is always trying to convince her to go, he is encouraging her to change. When he finds that she is finally going to change, he regrets the changes he forced upon her. The woman who didn't want to go before is now finding reasons to go. He has introduced her to a lifestyle that he really didn't want her to enjoy without him. Now he finds that she goes out all the time—without him. The next thing that happens is Mr. Right or Ms. Right walks up and starts making the woman laugh. The laughter opens her up to the possibilities of happier times and she starts thinking about all the things that are going wrong in her current relationship. These short but happy moments with other people who she meets are now causing unexpected problems in keeping her current relationship together. Now he regrets forcing her to change, but guess what? She loves the changes.

## DON'T GO THROUGH UNNECESSARY CHANGES

Once a woman finds out her man is cheating she should not take it personally. She should not go through unnecessary changes such as attempting to kill herself, or confront the other woman. When a man cheats it doesn't have a thing to do with the woman. It's all about his ego. It's best not to ask the kinds of questions that insinuate it's the woman who's weak or at fault because the relationship did not succeed. She should not ask, "What did I do wrong?," "Is she better than me in bed?," or any questions like that. A woman should get out of the relationship, get counseling, or allow the relationship to take its normal course. She should put her heart under lock and key until she decides it's safe to be free.

## NO ONE WANTS TO LOSE

Let's face facts . . . and look at it the correct way. No one wants to lose. I don't know a woman in the world who can handle rejection. If the man leaves, the woman feels rejected. If the woman leaves, the man feels he has lost a good woman. Somebody's got to win and somebody's got to lose.

## A MAN HAS TO WANT TO CHANGE

Women are beating themselves up trying to change men. Once something is inside a man, it's there until he decides to change it. She can do and say things that will make him consider changing, but there's nothing a woman can do to make a man change. She can make him want to cover it up, but there's nothing she can do to make this person change on the inside until he's ready to change. The best thing a woman can do to reduce stress in her life is stop trying to change a man into what she wants him to be and work more on herself. She might find that it's not him who needs to change, but something in her. A woman who tries to change a man before he is ready should understand . . . that's where her relationship mistakes begin and many of the problems start. A man feels that if he changes that one thing for her, the countdown begins. He feels that he will lose his own identity and he'll change so much that she won't want him anymore. He feels that she'll find somebody else and then become someone he doesn't know.

First of all, he's going to resist a woman who tries to change him, so instead of being what this woman wants him to be, he finds somebody who will let him be the person he really is. He begins to think that he no longer wants to put up with this kind of pressure, so he leaves. Now he starts looking for a woman who will understand "his need to be himself."

## WHEN A WOMAN IS TIRED OF THE MAN

People can tell when a woman is sick and tired of a man because of the things she does. Let's say something bad happens: a tornado comes through her town and she grabs her kids and starts to pray for everybody, except the man. She'll say, "Lord, please don't let anything happen to me and my children." The man hears her praying aloud and should recognize that she is tired of his mess. As a matter of fact she's so tired of him that she doesn't even consider adding his name to her prayers.

## CHECK YOUR LOVE SCALE

A woman can put her love on a scale. If his love is so heavy that it tips the scale in the right way, it's time for her to open her heart and release everything she's got inside of her to this man.

On the other hand if her scale is up and his is down, they shouldn't make another move. She has to be patient and give him a certain period of time to catch up. She can give him enough rope to hang himself, but she should not give him enough rope to tie her up or tie her down.

## WEIGH THIS THING OUT

Are you ready to make a change? If so, put all of the mess that you don't want to deal with on one side of the scale and all the good things that you want to deal with or do in life on the other side. Whichever one is the lightest, then that's what you go with. Everyone wants to go with what's heavy. They say, "I want to go with the heavy; I want the heaviest one." My advice is for women to go with the lightest load. You can throw all the rest of that stuff away. Just go upscale on everything you do. Deal with the other scale in life . . . the upscale life, which is usually the lightest load!

## MAKE SURE THE MAN CHANGES WITH YOU

If you are looking for a mate and you know that you've made some changes in your life, make sure the man goes along for the ride and changes with you. Make sure the changes you make will help you be better than you are today.

# Eighteen

# COMMUNICATION

*A woman should say what she means and mean what she says.*

If a man wants to communicate with a woman he'll come over to the woman in a gentlemanly way, introduce himself, and ask some questions that will let her know he's interested. He'll ask something like, "What's your name?" He'll say it in a way that lets the woman know he's interested in her. A woman has got to be patient, stop being desperate, looking desperate, and acting desperate for a man.

## COMMUNICATION MEANS TALKING
The thing that bothers men about some women . . . is how they go out there and marry, or I should say grab, a man with power. He's a man in the public eye, a man with money. She grabs him because she likes to see him with the power or she likes knowing that he's the man who everybody respects, but when it comes to home, she has somebody there who's quiet and doesn't want to talk to her about his problems. The strange thing is this

same person who won't talk to her can go out in public and talk all day.

What if Martin Luther King, Jr., never talked? What if Malcolm X never talked? What if the president never talked? We'd never get anywhere. There's got to be a way that a woman can have the same person at home who she has while in public. It's hard because once a man receives a lot of money, he thinks he's making the woman happy when he's spending money on her. It's fun at first and it'll probably last a few years, but once she discovers that she can buy anything she wants, she starts to change. Now she starts reaching back for the small things that she didn't get those few years that she was spending all the money. She realizes now that the money is not the most important thing.

## LET HIM TALK IT OUT

When a woman gets into an argument with a man, she should let him get all of his talk out and wait until he says all he has to say before she speaks. While he's talking she should be thinking of what she's going to say and do. Hopefully what she decides will be positive. Once he finishes and she says all she has to say she should simply walk away and be through with it. No matter what she's said or what he says she should be through with it. Then it's on him what happens afterward.

## WHAT SETS HER OFF SHUTS HIM DOWN

A man doesn't know what to say or when to say it to a woman because any little thing sets her off. When she is set off, he shuts down. Once he sets her off and she starts telling him what she thinks, the man backs down and lets her run her mouth. Once a man shuts down, it's hard to open that safe again. If the woman doesn't know the combination to get it open again—she's lost.

## BE CAREFUL OF WHAT YOU QUIETLY SAY TO YOURSELF

A woman not only has to be careful of what she says to people, she has to be careful of what she says about herself. It's very critical because what her inner voice says is what she feels. She plants the seed inside before it comes out of her mouth. Even though it's on the inside she's making the seed grow from all the negativity she's feeling.

## STOP TELLING PEOPLE YOUR BUSINESS

Quit telling other women your business. This includes your girlfriends. A woman should keep some things to herself. It's kind of like teaching someone to fight. If she teaches them every blow she knows, sooner or later they're going to end up fighting and then she won't have anything left to hit them with. They'll know the same moves she's going to make.

## WOMEN PLAY GAMES WITH WORDS

Women are always saying stuff to make men think they know what they are talking about. They have fine lines that they draw anywhere they want them to be. There's not a certain place she does it; she simply draws her line wherever she wants it to be. Once she draws that line she feels that the man is not supposed to cross it. As soon as the man thinks he knows where the line is the woman takes eight more steps and draws another one. Now, how in the world are men supposed to know what a woman is talking about?

## SMALL THINGS DO COUNT

To a woman it's the small things that count. Oh, she still wants the big things, but she wants the little things as well. She sees her girlfriends or her mom and they look like they are happy with it too, so she starts feeling like that's what's missing from her life. She's bought all the cars and everything she ever wanted. But it's the itty-bitty things she has to come back to. I guess because she was brought in this world with nothing and she was happy then. Maybe when she came out of the womb she was happy, but as she grew older she didn't know about all the things that could make her happier. She started getting greedy along the way and wanted more. It's the little things that people take for granted every day until tragedy happens in their lives. Maybe it was a bad accident and now she wishes she had her leg, her arm, or that she could get out of bed. It was nothing to get out of bed when she could, but when she can't get out, not even money can buy it. When money can't buy it she wishes she still had it. When money can't buy it God will still supply it.

## CLUB-WALKING WOMEN ARE JUST AS BAD AS STREET-WALKING WOMEN

When a woman goes clubbing with her friends she should quit walking around the club as if she's in a fashion show or modeling for a beauty pageant. A woman should set her watch and maybe take a stroll through the club once every forty-five minutes to an hour. In this way she will always look like a new person in the club. When a woman walks around every five minutes, men get tired of seeing her coming and going. Walking around frequently makes a woman appear immature or girlish. She should go to the ladies' room, update her makeup, check her appearance, walk back out, and sit down somewhere. Being seen too much is not a good thing. It's not flattering for the woman. A woman begins to look desperate and becomes old news to the men. By then the men just want the woman to get somewhere and sit her behind down.

## SAY WHAT YOU MEAN AND MEAN WHAT YOU SAY

A woman knows that one of the reasons men don't know what to do is because women will say one thing and mean another. Say, for instance, it's a holiday and she always wants to go to her mother and father's house. She disregards his parents and acts as if the man doesn't care anything about seeing his mama. She'll say, "We're over there all day on Sundays, what are we going over there for?" She should understand that his people want to see him too. Women are unfair about many things and then they wonder why the man builds up animosity toward her. It's because he's angry.

## WHAT DID YOU REALLY MEAN?

The woman will say, "Okay, this year we're going to get the kids something and we won't get each other anything." She'll say things like, "I don't need anything. I got everything I want." Then Christmas comes and the first thing out of her mouth is, "I know you haven't forgotten to buy me something." Then the man says, "I thought we said we weren't getting each other anything?" And she says, "You knew I didn't mean that." And he says, "How in the world was I supposed to know that?"

## TRY NOT TO USE THE WORDS "OR ELSE"

Don't use the words "or else." Don't give him an ultimatum or say things like:

"You better do this or else."
"Do it or else I'm going to leave."
"This is my last warning or else."

It appears that you're trying to make the man do something he doesn't want to do. That's when your relationship issues start. The man needs a lover, a friend, a mate—not another mother. You can't make someone love you, but you can make a person start hating you. It's so much better when you let your man do things for you and love you on his terms instead of trying to force what you want on your terms, with no consideration for your mate. Those words might temporarily fulfill your demands, but know that he is going to escape that whip and chain eventually.

## No Means No

An important word is *no*. Once a woman says "no more" a man should *not* move forward with what he was doing to her. Once she starts doing new things in her everyday life and stops doing what she did in the past, she begins to say "no more" more often. If she stops letting people do things to her, then she will get no more. People will see that you mean *no more*! If you say, "Okay, I'll give you one more time and you better not do it anymore 'cause if you do I'm going to do this or do that," they won't believe you're fed up and will keep testing your patience. No means no, so when you say "no more" you have to say it like you mean it.

## Is She Good Enough

I have a question for all women: What gives a woman the right to think that a man is supposed to treat her so well, cater to her, and take care of her? What makes her think she's good enough for that? Any questions? Yes? You want to answer that? Okay, I understand how you feel. You're talking to me bad. Now, I said all of that to get one point across. If a woman took that same energy that you just put against me, a person you don't know, and gave it to the man who's running over her, she could be somewhere else—with someone else—instead of being mistreated by him.

## Don't Resort to Cussing Your Man

It's not attractive for a woman to try and outcuss or cuss out her man. All she's doing is destroying her relationship. She is starting something she can't finish because cussing leads to something else, usually something worse. The disrespect that the two have for each other will definitely lead to anger, confusion, and tempers flaring. Once it starts, it's hard to stop. Even if he's cussing, the woman should try to maintain her dignity instead of standing against him toe to toe or cussing him.

## If God Is Missing in Your Life, You're Crippled

I think it's a beautiful thing when a woman meets a man who's crippled in some way and falls in love and marries him. It takes a very special person to do that and my hat goes off to her. I don't see anything lovely about a woman choosing a man for his looks and his money and not realizing he's crippled in other ways. You know a man is just as crippled when he doesn't have God in his life. When a man is crippled it's going to eventually cause some kind of communication problem in the relationship and it will definitely cripple the woman in some ways too.

## A Woman Should Be Careful of What She Says

It's all about watching what you say. A woman breathes in and what comes out of her mouth is important. She says, "I want a man who's rough," and that same roughneck she wished for can end up breaking her neck. Not only should she be careful of what she says, she should also be careful of what she asks for.

## Pay Attention to What's Happening Around You

Don't lighten up, tighten up. That's pretty important, to quit lightening up the load. Don't be a lightweight, but do tighten up and start paying more attention to what's happening to you. Sometimes women get where they start running with people, and they stop noticing their surroundings and things that are happening right before their eyes. They get so comfortable with friends that they think their life is all right. But they have to remember that their friend's life might be going in a different direction or maybe different things are happening for them. Women have to pay attention. This isn't a game out here and it's getting worse.

Here's a saying women should remember:

*As a rule man is a fool.*
*When it's hot he wants it cold.*
*When it's cold he wants it hot.*
*He always wants something he ain't got.*
—ANONYMOUS

SOMETIMES THE BEST COMMUNICATION IS TO BE QUIET
Sometimes a woman just needs to be quiet and she'll win the battle! If she wins the argument, then who really won the battle? Even if she won the argument she'll have hell in her house for the rest of her day.

# Nineteen

# LOVE

*It's difficult for a woman to find out that her man is having an affair with another woman. It's worse to find out that he's involved with more than one woman.*

*All right ladies, after you get hurt, I'll give you two or three days to drown in your sorrow, then you need to wake up and move on.*

Until a woman loves herself and God, her relationship with a man will never work. She can have an intimate relationship with a man, but it won't be right. There will be so much hell in her house and so many things going wrong that she would not believe. There will be one problem after another until she puts God in the mix. Also, until she loves herself and finds a man who is equally yoked, then and only then will she find peace.

## DEVELOP A LOVE CONNECTION

Plant a heavy kiss on his lips every morning and before he leaves put a love song on his mind. If you do that he'll say to himself at the end of his working day, "Let me get to my baby." Have a glass of wine waiting for him, and when you see him walking down the street make him feel he's someone special to meet. Develop a love connection with loving conversation full of soulful information. Don't ever be afraid to feel and touch him. Don't let your love life become routine. As the day turns to night you should excite his emotions. Let your mind let him know what you need.

## LOVE SONGS CAN HELP

I always listened to love songs. I would change the words to fit what I wanted to say so that I could get women. Once, I heard a candidate say something pretty slick on TV, so I turned it around and used it in the club. It worked on every woman I used it on. Here's how it went: I said it to one woman, "God gave Booker T. Washington books, He gave Billy D. Williams looks, He gave Sammy Davis Jr. shoes, and He gave B. B. King the blues. Of all the great things He gave and what I've seen Him do, I'm going to ask God to give me to you." She started blushing and saying, "Oh that was so sweet, you're so nice."

I remember when I was in Dallas, Texas, right after a Dallas Cowboys game. Everyone went out to the club and I wore a big cowboy hat, a belt with a huge buckle, some jeans, and a nice shirt. A young lady walked up to me and thought I was one of the players. All she kept saying was, "Oh my God, you're so big, are you a Cowboy?" I said, "Yes!" So she partied the rest of the night with me. After we left the club we stopped and got a bite to eat. We went to her place, had sex, and then the next morning we got up and went to breakfast. During the course of breakfast, she asked me, "What position do you play?" I said, "No! I'm not a Cowboy football player. I don't play football; I'm just a cowboy kind of cowboy." She was so hurt and angry with herself. That's one of the reasons I emphasize the importance of doing research before you part your legs. Trust your legs like a fire alarm. Don't set it off unless you know that you want a fire.

## YOU'LL NEVER HAVE THE MAN TO YOURSELF

I suggest women quit looking for the bling-bling all the time. Quit looking for the man who already has everything a woman wants because those are the guys a woman can't really have to herself. Of course, there are a few men who a woman can have to herself, but most of them are married. When a woman sees a guy with a nice car, diamonds and the like, she should sometimes look past it. If he has a brand-new Mercedes he also has brand-new Mercedes payments due. Then he has to try and get the house to go with the car. Women don't ever think about that. He might even have a brand-new Mercedes sitting in front of a little shotgun house, which should let a woman know the mentality of the man she's dealing with. If he does, he's the kind of guy who's thinking backward. A man should put more money into his home than he does his car. Oh, he might have bling-bling and a woman might even get a chance to ride around in his expensive car, and he might even spend money on her, or take trips with her, but she should ask herself if is he doing it in an honest way. These are tough questions, I know, but I'm trying to help women avoid being upside-down in more ways than one.

## LOVE CAN TURN INTO MISERY

Love hurts from time to time, but misery hurts twenty-four hours a day. That's how a woman can tell what she's gotten herself into. If a woman hurts some of the time and she feels good most of the time, she might be able to work it out. If a woman has misery all of the time, it's best for her to leave the relationship and move in a new direction. It's time for a new man and a new attitude.

## WHAT IS A WOMAN'S LEVEL OF LOVE?

I think the whole country is confused with the different levels of love. How many levels of love are there? So many people say love doesn't hurt. I'm not so sure about that because I know incidents where love has killed people. Love has given people ulcers. Love has given people heart attacks. Could that be considered as true love? Or is the woman a loving person 100 percent of the time and he only loves her 40 percent of the time? Does a woman give too much of her heart? Somebody needs to do a study on this and really break it down because I think the problem with love is the different levels. It's easy to say I love you, but come on, I love my sister, and I love my brother too. On what different levels does a woman love her kids or her parents? At what level does a person love? When does love make everything right enough that it doesn't hurt? Many times a woman doesn't know what to do because she's afraid. I know how love feels because I'm in love now, and it doesn't hurt. I've had women love me till no end, where they will take pills and try to kill themselves, but that might be foolish love too. What I used to do was let a woman love me all she could, then I chose what level of love I was going to give her back. My level of love would never be as high as hers. I always left enough room to jump out of the relationship when I got ready. I would leave the woman with the pain. I could always come and go as I pleased because I knew she still loved me so much that she would hurt when I wasn't around. I never had that level of love back then. When a woman doesn't love a man deeply, she can change her levels of love. When he gives more, she can give him more. Every time he ups his level, she should up hers, but if she runs out front and puts all of her love out there at the 100 point mark and he's not trying to go that far, she's going to have problems.

I used to say there's nothing I would do for a woman, now I'm saying there's nothing I wouldn't do for my wife.

# Twenty

# CHEATING

*New always seems good when it's new.*

When a woman finally picks the man she wants to be with she should lay some ground rules. She should inform him that if he cheats on her she's going to take some kind of action. That way it's wide open and even though he doesn't know her game plan he knows he'll have to deal with her if he cheats on her.

She should not give him any warnings like, "I'm going to leave if you cheat on me," because some men don't care. These kinds of threats only cause more problems. When a woman yells out, threatens to leave, or makes negative promises, it makes the dare factor come out in men. He dares her to leave. Empty threats make men angry and they react before the woman can act. The man often ends up leaving the woman just because she made threats to leave him and he doesn't want to be walked out on. Some men cheat so that the woman will leave.

A woman should be sure to keep her word if she promises that something will happen. If he cheats, something must surely happen. The one question I get asked more than any other is "Why do men cheat?" Here are several reasons why:

He can.
It's fun.
He's selfish.
He wants to see what he can make a woman do.
He wants to see how many women he can have.
He wants to see how much mess she can take off a man.
He wants to see what he can get away with.
He wants to practice some of his favorite sayings on women who he knows he wouldn't normally date.
He's insecure.

With so many answers to why men cheat, how in the world can a woman stop a man from cheating?

## MEN LIKE TO TRY SOMETHING NEW

The bottom line is, new always seems good when it's new. A woman likes new just as much as a man, but a man likes new relationships whereas a woman relies on the familiar. For the woman new is like a new pair of shoes she can't wait to get on, but once her feet begin to hurt she reaches back for her comfortable and familiar ones.

## IF A WOMAN CATCHES HER MAN CHEATING

A woman will sometimes kick her man out because he cheated. Every woman should remember that there's always another woman out there who will want him. It might be the one woman he's cheating with who can see the better qualities in him that his lover is too blind to see. The strange thing is that once the woman kicks him out she'll oftentimes try to get him back because she can't find anyone better than him.

## Talking Can Lead to Cheating

I remember talking to a young lady in the club one night. She was sitting alone and listening to the band. I thought I'd ease up over there and say something to her. Just when I started talking to her, I introduced myself and she said, "How are you doing?" I said, "I wonder if I can sit here for a few minutes and talk to you. I got a few things I want to ask you." She said, "No thank you, I came out to hear a little music and I'm going back home, so whatever you're going to say, I'm sorry but I have no use for it." It made me angry, but I said, "Okay, cool," and walked away. At the same time it turned me on because I'm thinking, Man, this is the way I would want my wife to be. But of course, most women want to sit there and see what the man is all about before they judge which way to treat him. She'll try to see if he's better than the man she already has and if he's not, she runs him off, but if he is, she sits there, laughs, and talks like there's nothing wrong with it. She uses the excuse of "We're just talking." She then gives the man her phone number if he wants it and the cheating begins. Talking is where everything starts.

## A Man's No Really Means Yes When It Comes to Sex

Women ask, "Why are men so weak? Why they can't be strong like women when somebody is trying to flirt with them or offer them sex?" Women get this offer from men more often than a man gets it from a woman. Men are always asking women for sex, but a woman rarely asks a man for sex. "Does a man really want to have sex every time?" Most times yes, but even when he says no it sounds more like a yes than a no. That's why a man has to think twice before he says yes or no because it's been a long time since somebody asked him if he wanted to have sex.

## MARRIED WOMEN WHO CHEAT

Married women are cheating in record numbers. A woman should not sell her soul like that. A woman who cheats doesn't really get payback for the man who cheats on her. Her best payback is to leave and go on with a better life. It shouldn't be considered payback when a woman messes around just because the man is messing around. Where does God come into her life? Somewhere it has to kick in and she has to say, "This isn't what God would want me to do; I'm doing it because that's what I want." The guy she's cheating with feels good to her because he's new. But as she gets to know him, like the man she's cheating against, it's going to be pretty much the same thing. She should try to work it out because there's a happy median in there where two people can come together and talk. If she can't work it out she should just be gone.

## IF A MAN CONTINUES TO CHEAT

When a woman finds that her man has cheated over and over again, she should end the relationship because he has shown that he is always going to cheat. A woman should find a man who's going to respect her.

## IF A WOMAN CHEATS OVER AND OVER AGAIN

The cycle repeats itself. Now a woman has put herself in the whore category because she's with multiple men, yet she still considers herself a one-man woman. The woman becomes similar to a doorknob (every one gets a turn) and she still denies being a whore. A woman who goes from man to man trying to find one who won't cheat soon finds that she is really the one who's sleeping around.

## ANGER FROM A WOMAN WHO'S BEEN CHEATED ON

When a woman is angry she will do things that she shouldn't do. She destroys his property, breaks his windows, cuts his tires, and watches what he does and where he goes. She stalks him before she realizes what she's doing. In legal terms she *is* stalking!

## HOLDING ON TO A CHEATING MAN

A lot of times a woman will try to hold on to a man once she catches him cheating because she's embarrassed and she doesn't want to feel like anyone beat her out, but if she's trying to hold on to him for the wrong reason she's only cheating herself.

I hope that the information I'm putting out here helps someone. If each one of us would reach one, then teach that one, the world would be a better place.

# Twenty-One

# CAREERS

*When a woman takes valuable time out of her life to start doing things for a man, she's actually putting her life on hold.*

Whatever a woman does for a living she should make sure it's what God gave her as her craft. The gift that God gave her won't get her passion mixed up with her gift. Some women think cheating on men and selling their behind is a gift. She thinks that her stuff is so good that it's what God gave her as her gift. What she doesn't know is that it's not a gift and it's really not that good. She can give it away—to men who don't require much.

### DO YOU KNOW IF HE'S MAKING AN HONEST LIVING?

Does he have a W-2? Does his job show that he's making the kind of money to afford the things he's buying? How is he living? Does he live in a low-rent area and drive a high-income vehicle? A woman should do a check on the man. When it's time for him to show he's doing it honestly she might find out that nine out of ten times he's doing something wrong to get the things *she* holds so dear. Getting involved with a man who's getting his possessions the wrong way can get a woman in trouble.

## DON'T PUT YOUR LIFE ON HOLD

A woman can be on the right track, but when she meets a man and takes the time she was putting into her own project and gives that time to the man, she sets herself back. If he walks away from her, she's further behind than when she started. When a woman takes valuable time out of her life to start doing things for a man, she's actually putting her life on hold.

## SOME MEN DON'T KNOW HOW TO SETTLE DOWN

Some men have partied, met hundreds of women, and they feel like they've already done everything, so they are ready to settle down. Settling down is brand-new to many men and they don't know how to do it or handle the idea of commitment. They want it because they've never done it before, but once they try to settle down they find they are not ready. A man finds that he has decided to settle down with the wrong woman, so he falls off the wagon and begins to do the things that a man who has not settled down does. Once a woman gets a good man—one who is willing to settle down with her—and she determines this is the man she wants to be with, life can be good. The settled man is happy because he loves his woman and the comforts of his home. He loves it so much that he hates to get up and go somewhere or run errands. He enjoys being at home with his woman.

To get something that you never had you have to do something that you never did.

# Twenty-Two

# MONEY

*Until a woman is living the life she wants to live she should always put some money away just in case things don't work out as planned.*

*Every woman needs a stash so that if she has to leave in a hurry, she has a means of survival.*

A woman who dates for money gets to live in a big house, drive a fancy car, wear designer clothes, dine at the best restaurants, and feel that everything is good. Once that same woman sees that the man has issues that cause him to be borderline crazy, she realizes that she's made a big mistake, but she stays with him pretending that everything is okay. She does this because her girlfriends have seen her at the top of her game. She doesn't want to leave him because leaving him would disrupt her life and her financial situation. A woman looks at her situation and can see it as the ultimate relationship even though she's getting abused and misused by this guy. She goes through the pain anyway because she doesn't want to give up their material possessions. Once the relationship is over and she has to move into an apartment or a smaller house, she's afraid to hear her girlfriends say, "Ha, ha, look at her now! She's not all that after all."

## QUIT BEING A GOLD DIGGER

Once you care about somebody, quit thinking about expensive gifts. Quit dating and asking for big gifts and start asking the man for a big heart with big hugs. Let him decide what to get you and how much to spend on you. A woman should go for the love, not the gifts. What happens to couples is that they start giving so many other things that they forget to give of themselves. Once you start giving back yourself, that's priceless. I don't know anything that can pay for what's inside of a man or woman. There's seldom a person who you want to give yourself to completely. When you give yourself, be happy and be proud that you're giving yourself to the man you desire. Do it from your heart and out of your soul.

## EVERY WOMAN SHOULD PUT SOME MONEY AWAY

Until a woman is living the life she wants to live she should always put some money away just in case things don't work out as planned. If things do work out, then she'll have money to put with what she already has. A woman should always have some money in a place that is reserved for dire emergencies. We'll call it her stash because a woman might just need it to get away.

## QUIT WORRYING ABOUT MONEY SO MUCH

Don't let money make you. You should make the money.

A woman always think that someone has stolen her man's heart. A heart can never be stolen; it simply goes where it wants to go.

# Twenty-Three

# SEX

*Once a woman falls in love how will she know the man will catch her?*

*Open your heart before you open your legs.*

Hold off on the sex. It's easier to get money and commitment from a man who you *haven't* had sex with than to get it from a man you had sex with. Why? Because the man and the woman both feel like they have something invested and they tend not to let the relationship slip away so easily when they haven't had sex. They have that part of the relationship to look forward to.

## SATISFY MORE THAN ONE OF YOUR NEEDS
A woman should seek a man who can satisfy her in more ways than one. He should be able to:

1. Communicate with her on her level and then some.
2. Fulfill some of her desires.

3. Share in the things she likes to do in wholesome and positive ways.
4. Get along with some of her relatives.
5. Join her in spiritual gatherings.
6. Feel comfortable in public and in private with her.

The more needs he can satisfy, the more chances of the relationship being successful.

## FIFTY-FIFTY RELATIONSHIP

Once you meet a man and release your body to him for the first time, you have already reduced your chances of getting a good relationship. It's now only a fifty-fifty chance. A woman's leverage is now different than it was when she started the relationship. Before he knew anything about her the chances were better. When a woman releases her body to a man the tables are turned because he's already gotten what he was after. The woman hopes he likes her after she's had sex with him, but the conversations get noticeably shorter and she might look up and see him running around with someone else.

## PLACES NOT TO GO IF SHE DOESN'T WANT SEX

Something is bound to happen if you go where you shouldn't. If you don't want to have sex, don't:

Go into a man's bedroom.
Go into his hotel room.
Get in the back seat of his car.
Go to an empty parking lot.
Go to a secluded area.
Go into his home for a drink.

Invite him into your house.

Accept invitations for a late-night stayover unless you are ready to part your legs.

These are all invitations to have sex and once a man gets started he forces the rest of his way in. He sees, hears, and feels everything is acceptable, even if the woman says or feels that it's not. Men will quit when a woman says stop, but deep down in his loins he doesn't think that the woman really means stop.

## SATISFACTION WITH A MAN

If the woman is trying to get her freak on by having a one-night stand or just kicking it, she should go ahead and get all she can to satisfy herself. If she's picking a man who has the potential to be her husband, she should hold back on being a freak, even if she is one. Men don't want to be with a woman who looks like she's been with everyone and has learned everything already and is liberal with his sexual appetite early in the relationship.

## A WOMAN SHOULD LEARN TO SATISFY HERSELF

Before a woman seeks satisfaction outside of herself she should learn to love the stranger within. A woman expects a man to be a man and she also expects to be respected by him. It's so difficult for a woman to find a good man to satisfy her because she doesn't know what satisfies her. A good man is always hard to find. Until she finds him she needs to learn how to satisfy herself. It might be a long search. When he comes knocking she can lay the path for him and be able to please him.

## IF YOU'RE A FREAK UNDERCOVER

If you want to break loose on your man, give him a little freak at a time. Little by little play sex tapes, sex videos, and do sexual things that please him. You can release the pussycat within. If a woman is watching a sex movie she should observe it for a while before suggesting any of the games. When the people in the film do something that she thinks she might like, she should ask him if he'd like to try it. Doing it this way leaves the man with his pride and the illusion that he turned her out. If she does too many things to him sexually on the first sexual encounter he'll think she knows too much and he might just turn away from her. A man doesn't want to think that his woman knows too much about sex in the beginning. He might think she's been sleeping around. He doesn't want to be with a woman who's been with lots of men or knows everything about sex unless she's a hooker or their relationship is seasoned and he feels they learned it together.

## KEEP YOURSELF TOGETHER

If a woman breaks the rule and has sex with a man the first night, she should wake up the next morning before he does and freshen her makeup. She should put on a pair of high heels and her housecoat, and get her legs looking good. When he leaves he'll feel the same way as when he came. He'll think that the woman is so fine because when a woman is in high heels; her legs look like she's working out. They look very nice and toned. Try not to wake up in the morning looking crazy. It's too early in the morning and in the relationship for him to see you looking a mess.

Looking for a good woman is like looking for a house. If I gave you five hundred thousand dollars cash to buy a house, you would automatically look at at least ten to fifteen houses before you made a selection. You would decide on the house you wanted with some criteria in mind. "No, this kitchen isn't big enough, I don't like the bathroom in there. No, the living room isn't big enough." That's the same way men judge and select women. Women should know that men have difficulty trying to select a mate out from all the available ones. It's like trying to find a house where every part is right, so when he walks in he'll be saying, "I'll take this one, it's perfect."

## SEX: GOING ON A DATE FOR THE FIRST TIME

When a woman knows that she's going to have sex with a man, she should make sure . . .

- It's for her and not him.
- She needs it more than he does.
- Her mind and heart look at it in the same way.

She might say to herself, "Well, it doesn't make any difference whether I talk to him or not, because I sure needed that." The woman shouldn't even look for the man to call her the next day, but if he does, she might have a man worth thinking about. On the flip side, she shouldn't get angry because he didn't call her after she got what she wanted. If he contacts her and says he wants to see her again or he wants to get to know her better, then and only then should she move forward with the relationship.

## SEX HELPS MEN OPEN UP TO WOMEN

Women should be aware that for a man, sexual arousal helps him connect with and realize how he feels about a woman. It is through good sex that a man starts to open his heart, allowing him to experience feelings that help him determine if the woman has more substance and staying power. If she's the kind of woman who will have the man's back and really proves to him that she wants him just as much as he wants her, she'll receive both his loving feelings and his hunger for love. Of course a man can feel loved in other ways, but the most powerful way a woman's love can touch a man's soul and open his heart is through great sex. The closest a man can ever get to a woman is inside of her. Not with hugging, kissing, or through intense conversation, but inside of her. It's like riding around in your car just looking at the woman's house; he'll never know what's going on until he gets inside.

## A WOMAN NEEDS TO FEEL NEEDED

As the relationship grows and things cool down a woman needs good communication from the man to feel loved continuously. Receiving love helps a woman fulfill her need and hunger for sex.

Because a man often misunderstands a woman's real need for romance, he may not understand her mood swings. He instead feels she is withholding sex. He doesn't realize that the need to feel needed and cared for helps a woman get in the mood. When a couple is experiencing relationship problems, sometimes instead of focusing on fixing the problem they tend to take shortcuts and stir up passion that creates great moments, which increases the desire to be with each other and eventually have sex—thinking it will make the problems easier to solve. The couple has sex again and the work to break the cycle begins all over again.

## BE CAREFUL OF WHAT MEN SAY TO YOU

When the guys are sitting around saying things like, "Boy, look at the butt on her," that turns many women off, but some women are turned on. You've got to be careful of who's saying it to you. It might be someone desperate who will mess with anything and have no class and then it's not a compliment. Be very careful about the compliments you receive, because in nine out of ten the man simply wants sex.

## THREESOMES

Somewhere down the line a man will sometimes ask his woman to do a threesome. It might sound fun and exciting, but sooner or later the threesome will turn into a twosome and someone will be left out. Don't let it be you. If what you're trying to do is please your man, I wouldn't advise you to do a threesome, and if you are doing it, I advise you to stop.

## A MAN'S LIFE CAN BE RUINED IN
## A MOMENT OF WEAKNESS

A man's life can be ruined in a moment of weakness. When a man decides to have sex with a woman or have a relationship with her and he's weak, he surrenders to her. Now he's got AIDS and his wife has found out he had a relationship on the side. Because of this, his relationship with his wife and kids is ruined. Now the man's life is gone because of a moment of weakness.

## MEN BUYING PORNO BOOKS

So what if a man has a few porno books in the bathroom or somewhere around the house. Women should quit getting mad at this. Even if he does something that she doesn't approve of, like taking care of himself sexually, when she gets on him, he says, "I'm just doing what I have to do."

Quit getting mad at him. Many women would rather he did that than have him do what he wants to do or really can do. At least he's by himself. What does she really want? It's as if women don't take care of themselves sexually when nobody's around. A few women will say they don't and there are women who admit they have never done it, but there are more women who do it than those who don't.

## STOP WORRYING ABOUT THE OTHER WOMEN

Women very often wonder if the other woman is better than she is in bed. A woman should not worry herself to death about what another woman can do sexually to please a man. If a man and a woman agree to try something new, then it's cool, but for a woman to just look at a bunch of stuff and say she's going to try that on her man does not make him care more for her. It may work for a little while, but he's going to eventually ask, "Where did you learn that?"

## SEX CAN'T SAVE A RELATIONSHIP

You're watching a sex film and you're trying to find a position to put yourself in. You're going back and forth, twisting your ankles and trying to come up with new ways to please him and now he wants to know where you learned it. What makes sex good in a relationship is how the person feels about you. If that man loves you until the end of his time, the sex is going to be good. If he's tired of you and hates you, I don't care how many sexual positions you put yourself in, it's not going to be all that good to him. He knows that a new woman is going to be good to him just because she's new.

## I CAN'T GET NO SATISFACTION

A young lady asked me how to get her man to fully satisfy her. She says he's doing great in bed, but she would like him to add a few things that she felt would satisfy her more. She didn't want to tell him that he's not doing it right. Of course he's doing many of the things right, but some additional things would really make the situation better. I suggest a woman do it in a heated moment of passion. She should not tell him because men don't like to be scolded. They feel like the woman is scolding him or saying he doesn't know what he's doing when all she has to do is sit down with him and talk face to face. A woman should wait until the sex act begins, then tell the man what she wants. She should act as if she can't take it by falling off the bed and making a big deal out of the whole thing. She should make him feel like it's the greatest thing ever and then he'll always go back to that spot because he'll think this is what really flips her over—so he can be the man.

The mere appearance of being a loose woman can turn a potential husband off.

# Twenty-Four

# DOWN LOW

*A down-low girl is a bonus for men because she's bringing another woman to the table and men love that.*

We've heard about the down-low brothers, but no one is saying anything about the down-low girls. Some men enjoy having one because everyone else is discussing the down-low men. I'd like to discuss the down-low women. What's wrong in one person's life might be right in another's. When a man meets a down-low girl he's all right with it. She's a bonus for the man because she's bringing another woman to the table and men love that. If a woman decides to become down-low, she'd better be careful—it could be more trouble than she thinks.

## YOU DON'T HAVE TO GO THROUGH THE PAIN

I have lived fifty years of a pretty challenging life, straight street and lots of competition. I've lived through most anything that can happen to a person. I've never been homeless, but I've been without a home. I've had many women and always had a place to stay, but I didn't have anywhere to live. When you live in times like these your car becomes your closet and after staying a couple of nights in there you start considering it a pleasure instead of a burden. I don't know anything about down-low men so I can't help you in that department. There are many books written by brothers on this subject; you can go to Google and find various titles.

# Twenty-Five

# ETIQUETTE

*Don't lower your standards to get the man you want because most men don't know what they want.*

A woman should keep her home clean. If she's going to have company and her man is coming over, she should make sure her presentation is up to par. Men adore clean women and they love women who take the time to make sure everything about their home is clean. A woman should clean the house thoroughly because he might be looking to keep her and wants to make her his wife. When a woman is nasty, junky, or dirty, it will probably turn the man off or scare him away. "Clean is as clean does."

## TAKE CARE OF YOURSELF

A woman can only hurt a man one time and he'll move on. If the woman doesn't take care of herself and she starts looking bad and ungroomed, he'll start looking at other women who are cleaner and neater. If the relationship is on the brink and the woman ends up seeing the man out somewhere, the first thing he'll think is, "I took care of you better than you took care of yourself." No man should ever be able to think he can take care of a woman better than she can take care of herself. Women have got to stay on top of their game.

## DON'T LOWER YOUR STANDARDS JUST TO GET A MAN

No woman has to lower her standards to get the man she wants. Most men don't know what they want and it could possibly be you. Don't holler at a man or come on to a man. All the woman has to do is be in the vicinity of the man and let him holler at her.

## FOLLOW HIS LEAD

If the woman is out with a man at an event she should simply follow his lead. He won't be able to chill, become laid-back, and act cool if his woman isn't cool. Being loud, drinking too much, and putting on a show only causes unnecessary friction. She should just chill out and be as smooth as he's trying to be. She should make him proud and have everyone saying she's such a lady. People know the difference between a lady and a girl. Nonclassy women can't fool people. The man wants to show her off but won't like it if she is loud and puts on a show.

## DO NOT TELL THE NEW GUY ABOUT OTHER GUYS IN YOUR LIFE

If a woman must say anything it should be, "I haven't been an angel all my life." She can let him know she's been through a few changes that she didn't like, but she should never tell him how many guys she has slept with. A woman should not discuss any particular guy because every time her lover sees the guy he's going to say something about him or compare her love against this guy. He will worry about the other guy and probably make statements like, "You still want him, don't you?" "Why are you looking at him like that?" She should be careful what she says to her man about another man. It only brings bad feelings and room for unnecessary discussion.

## GET RID OF THE GHETTO MENTALITY

A lady does not fight! She talks her way out of situations. When confronted by another woman all she should do is say, "I'm sorry" and "Excuse me," and then go on about her business. Fighting will only get a woman's face scratched up and when a man meets her, he'll want to know what happened. He'll ask, "Where did you get those scratches from?" And when she has to answer, and if she tells the truth, she'll say, "I was fighting." How does that sound to the man who's interested in you?

## PUBLIC ETIQUETTE WHEN YOU'RE OUT

When you're out in public don't chew gum. Take the gum out of your mouth; even better, take it out of your purse. When a woman chews gum she looks like a big cow chewing grass. If she needs to freshen her breath she should use breath mints instead. Breath mints help her look more ladylike too.

## PERSONAL CARE

Hygiene and grooming are very important for a woman, even if she's down to her last penny. If her nails are chipped, her hair is not lined, and she has no makeup on, the man will be less likely to approach her. The more she looks like she's having a hard time, the harder her times will get. Society will label her and place her in a corner. If a woman looks like she's going somewhere and doing positive things with her life, the man will be willing to help her. People will help a person who looks like they have money more than they will a homeless person who doesn't have anything, because they believe they can come back later and ask for a favor in return. But a homeless person or someone who doesn't have any-thing, there's nothing they can do for them.

## DON'T LET YOUR "UPKEEP" BE YOUR DOWNFALL

A woman should not spend her whole life or her budget trying to keep herself made up. She should not work so hard to dress nice, go to church, pay her own bills, and then settle for a man who doesn't have a job or doesn't care anything about God.

## DON'T LOOK BACK

Women look back too much. Looking back ruins a woman's ability to step forward. For example, try to walk backward and then deter-mine how long you can do it. We all know that humans are not de-signed to walk backward. Of course, we can go in reverse with our bodies and walk backward, but my question is, "How long can you do it comfortably?" It was meant for us to go forward because it's our natural motion. When you start walking backward, watch how fast you get tired. The reason I bring this scenario to you is because women need to quit going backward in their life. If a woman knows that she's tired of going backward, she should begin working on a plan to move forward. *Quit rehearsing your reverse.* As a matter of fact take the reverse gear out of your body. Trying to reminisce and think about old times isn't good for anyone. A woman thinks, "Re-member that guy I used to date named Johnny? Remember how much fun I used to have. Remember how we were so close and we did so many things together?"

I hate to be the one to tell her this, but those days are long gone. If the woman didn't save that moment and try to keep that man, she has to realize . . . it's gone, finished, done with. She should move forward and try to have good days with someone else. Instead she's trying to reach back and look at the past because it makes her feel like he was the man God chose for her. Now she's trying to find him. She'll ask all his cousins and friends, "Have you seen him? Where is he?" Of course they'll tell her, "He's married now." Then she'll say, "Girl, that doesn't mean anything to me. I can still get him." Now, why would she take herself through that? A woman should quit putting pressure on herself! She should release herself. All she has to do is let go and let God.

## How's He Living?

When a woman visits a man's home and she sees other guys living there, she should ask why. If he tells her it helps pay rent, know that he is not ready to take care of a household. When you see he has a nice business card and an expensive car, but is still splitting rent with four other guys, maybe his business is not going so good and he's really living a lie.

## Take Care of Yourself

When a woman says, "He should take me like I am," she's narrowing her options. Women who say that are guilty of being lazy. It takes work to shine up your presentation, but it pays off. You feel better when you put a little effort into yourself. No man wants to look at a woman's nappy head and dusty scalp. I've met women who say, "I'm a natural woman." The man says, "You'd better get in there and do what's natural . . . comb your hair, put on some makeup, and get yourself together." Put on some clean clothes that fit and appeal to the man. No man wants to walk around or be seen with a woman who doesn't take care of herself or her hygiene. It's difficult to catch a man who's trying to do something with his life and has a woman who won't take care of herself. He's simply not attracted to that kind of woman.

## WHOEVER INVITES PAYS FOR THE DATE

If a woman calls a man and invites him on a date, she should not expect the man to pay for it. The rule of thumb is, whoever does the inviting should pay for the date. This is normal operating procedure unless it is decided early on that both will pay for the date. Be sure to make it clear ahead of time what's going on and who's going to do what.

I was a man who always had a job and a lot going for him. I could use women more freely than a man who didn't have a job.

Be forewarned: If a woman throws a good man away and tries to find a diamond in the rough, he might be rougher than she thinks.

# Twenty-Six

# DRESSING RIGHT

*A woman doesn't have to give in to showing skin just to get a man.*

I don't know why women have it in their heads that if they show more skin they'll get more. It doesn't look good when a woman shows so much of her body that the man can see more skin than clothes. Sometimes it's so revealing that the woman looks sleazy. Some single men think it's cool, but if he's looking for a wife or someone to take care of, he doesn't want that kind of woman in his house. If he wants to look like he's a single man, he'll keep her around just to kick it with her. She'll never really get to be the wife if she reveals too much of herself or her body. Now there are exceptions to the rule, but "to show more is to get more" is out of the question. Show less and you'll get the best! The quality of man that a woman gets when she shows too much skin is a man seeking sexual pleasure.

## DRESS PROPERLY FOR THE OCCASION

I saw a woman walking down the street with a miniskirt on, midriff-baring top, rings in her nose and eyebrows, holes in her stockings, run-down shoes, smoking a cigarette, with unruly hair that was held together by a dirty rubber band, yet she's looking for a job and wants someone to hire her. This woman would rather look inappropriate and try to catch a man than look presentable for a job interview. She should know that if she takes care of herself and gets the job she can acquire some of the things she wants. She'll also have a better chance at getting a man who meets her improved standards.

No man wants to walk around or be seen with a woman who doesn't take care of herself or her hygiene. Presentation is essential.

# Twenty-Seven

# ADVICE

*Don't ever be afraid to lose. If you face fear it will disappear.*

When a woman is looking at a man for all of the wrong reasons and trying to get the wrong things, she becomes blind. Sometimes she lets her good sense get in the way of her common sense and she misses the obvious red flags. Women need to use more common sense. It will take them a lot further.

## GET SOME CONFIDENCE FIRST
A young lady asks me for advice all the time. She told me she wants to find a man who can help her with her shortcomings—someone she can call her confidant. My answer to her is until you can get some confidence you can forget about the confidant.

## I DO WHAT FEELS RIGHT
When I work toward making a decision I always do what I want no matter who tells me what to do. I can live with my decision. If I listen to someone else and go out of my way to do what they say and

it's supposed to be the right way, but it doesn't turn out right, I'm going to be mad as hell for the rest of my life at that person. But if I make it up in my mind that this is what I'm going to do and it doesn't turn out right, I can live with it. I'm cool with it, because then it's my mistake.

## ARE YOU AN EVIL WOMAN?

Some women are so evil. They can't seem to get along with anybody. She's so bad she doesn't even realize that she can't get along with herself. If she can't get along with herself how does she expect to get along with anybody else? Are you an evil woman?

## DON'T TRY TO BE BIG-TIME

A friend of mine wanted some advice. He has a little money now, because somebody passed away and left it to him. I simply told him, "Don't try to be big-time with your little money and end up broke."

## DON'T BE A FOOL . . . FOOL!

I used to make women cook me dinner and when we got home I would invite another girl over to eat the dinner. Stuff like this is what makes a woman a fool for a man. Women have got to stop letting men do them this way.

## HER FIRST MAN IS HER STEPPING-STONE

Life is one big growing pain. A woman will never keep the man she started with. Only one in a million will keep the first man. A woman must understand that she has to graduate or she'll remain stuck on stupid. The man she started with is just her stepping-stone.

## DON'T GET THINGS CONFUSED

We all do foolish things when we're angry. Because we know that anger is inappropriate, a woman has to realize that she shouldn't let love turn her into an angry person. I'm not trying to be mean, but I am asking women to stop, drop, and roll before they do something stupid. When you get so angry that you think of doing something stupid, act like your behind is on fire. Imagine a woman who's killed somebody and now she's gone to the penitentiary. She killed, got caught, and now she's doing her time in jail. That's painful, having to do forty years or fifty years just because she got angry one day. Don't get it confused. The message for women is don't get *making love* confused with love. They are two different things. If you love a man for the kind of sex he puts down, that's not love, that simply means you're addicted and horny and want to be physically satisfied. Don't get love confused with how he makes you feel in bed and how he makes you feel as a whole person.

Don't tear a man down verbally, just move on. Maybe with a few repairs he'll be good for someone else.

# Twenty-Eight

# FIGHTING

*It's a dumb move on a woman's part when she brings family mem-
bers, outsiders, friends, or children into fights with her lover.*

When a woman gets into a squabble with her man—she's
fought him, cursed him, and is on bad terms—she shouldn't
get her family members involved. Don't go get Pooky, Leroy, and
Bubba, because you're only setting them up to get in trouble and
end up in jail with a court case because you couldn't handle what
you started. When a woman falls out with her man in the heat of
anger and brings other people into her mess, it never turns out the
way she thinks. She picked the man, now she's bringing others in
her disagreements to help handle him, and most times a man is not
to be handled. She should just let it go. It's a bad move, it's a dumb
move, and it's an idiot move on a woman's part when she brings
family members, outsiders, friends, or children into her fights with
her lover. If she must call someone, she should call the police. It's
their job to handle disputes and domestic problems. They're
trained to handle it in the best way. Most times family members act
on their emotions whereas the police act on jurisdiction, and from a

neutral point of view. Why get family members involved in the matter? It's usually because the woman is hurting so bad she wants him to hurt. A man might never lift a hand to fight a woman, but when it's time for him to defend himself from another man or family member, he fights back with a vengeance.

## CALL THE POLICE AND TALK TO GOD

There are three things that can get a man so upset that he'll get up and start moving around.

1. When a woman calls her brother. Her brother might even scare the man.
2. When she calls the police. No man wants to go to jail.
3. When she tells him that she's going to talk to God about him.

Tough guys really don't want to deal with these three things. They talk noise like they will, but they really don't want you to call the police or talk to God!

## DON'T MAKE A MAN FIGHT

Sometimes a woman will meet a man and know that he doesn't want her, but she falls for him anyway. She's not there for him and he's not there for her, but she falls for him anyway. She should stop making men fight her and instead make them think she's worth fighting for. When a man does something wrong she has to ask God to forgive him, then she has to forget him and move on if she doesn't want him anymore. Don't tear him down, just move on. Maybe he's good for someone else.

## I Made Women Fight with Themselves

There were times when I didn't care. I would act a fool instead of fight with a woman. Knowing I'm six feet seven inches tall and 350 pounds, I would give women weapons or have them dial the numbers 91 just to make them feel it was an equal fight. All they had left to dial was the final 1. But then I would throw them off by saying, "You'd better kill me because if you don't, you're going to have a problem." I learned that very few women would try to kill a fool. If she didn't kill me, she didn't want to deal with the consequences of her actions or my threats. During these times in my life I would give the woman a gun, load it, pull the trigger, cock it back, put it in her hand and against my head, then slap her so she would have a reason to hurt me. I would make it easy for her to shoot me. Anytime she felt like she was in harm's way she could pull the trigger. I know that sounds crazy, but that's where I was in my life. Sometimes I would take a butcher knife, put it in a woman's hand, aim it at my chest, and slap her. Women would just throw the gun or the knife down, and then would cry because they were so scared of me that they wouldn't kill me. And trust me ladies, I didn't want to be crazy. My heart didn't, but my mind did.

That's where people put me. I had to hold that standard up so they wouldn't think less of me. It was a catch-22 situation. People accepted that I was crazy. They would say things like, "He's crazy." "Ah, he's just that way." And right today I refuse to let anyone violate me or be a certain way with me because that's just the way I am. I want women to have enough strength to say, "Hey, stop." She has to put her foot down at some point because it's a stopping point for everybody. Everybody thinks it's the tough guy who wants to be the baddest man in the world. Somewhere in his heart he wishes he were out of all that mess. He doesn't know his way out because people won't let him out. It's the tough guy who wants to come in, but a woman won't let him in.

## I'M ASHAMED OF THE THINGS I DID

I'm not bragging. I'm ashamed of the things I did, but God is giving me an opportunity to use it as a teaching tool—so there's a window of positive opportunity in it. I thought what I was doing was right until God slapped me. And guess what, God's hand is way bigger than mine. Ask God to never let you meet a man who'll take you through these kinds of changes, and please, focus on the lessons in this book. Don't just look at what I've done in the past. Look at how I've changed for the better.

## ABUSIVE MEN COME IN ALL TONES

Let's say a woman has met a man and he's all right. He seems to be a nice guy and she gives him her phone number, but she doesn't really want to talk to him all day or every day so when he calls she doesn't return his call. He calls her the next day and she doesn't return his call. Watch how the anger builds up. That's how she'll know she's got a crazy man on her hands. First he says, "Hi, I called you the other day and I didn't really want anything. I just thought you were a nice lady and I wanted to see you again." The next day the message says, "Hey, I don't know if you got my message the other day, but I called you." And on the third day, he says, "Maybe you're out of town or something and you haven't received my message, but I'm trying to reach you because I wanted to holler at you." The fourth day: "Ah, look here, don't play games with me. See, you could have told me you weren't going to take my call. You didn't have to put me through all this." His tone lets the woman know he's crazy from the beginning and he's probably going to be crazy in the end. The best thing she can do is stay away from him. Don't even think of having a relationship with him.

## ARE YOU WITH THE WRONG MAN?
Ladies, I'm not saying that with all the stuff I've done to women you're supposed to stay with a man and get abused and beat up. I'm trying to say there's good inside every person, man or woman. It doesn't take a rocket scientist to understand that if a woman is catching hell and getting abused, she's with the wrong person. It takes a certain woman to pull the good out of a man. A woman should find the man that God has for her and then receive the goodness that's inside of that man.

Sometimes a woman needs to be a quiet storm just to win the battle. A woman is on her way to recovery once she realizes that it wasn't the man who tricked her, but she tricked herself because of love.

# Twenty-Nine

# LEAVING

*When you say, "He makes my heart skip a beat" it might be because your brain is trying to tell you to run.*

What the man finds out when he wants a woman to leave is that he can't get her to leave. When the woman knows that the man doesn't care she will sit there and keep putting herself on him, trying to make him care because she doesn't want to lose him. She especially doesn't want to lose him to another woman. If another woman is involved she fights for him in all the wrong ways. She fights to stay with this man even though she knows he doesn't really want her to stay.

## INFORM THE OTHER MAN WHEN
## THE RELATIONSHIP IS OVER

If the woman wants to end the relationship and go into another one with someone else, she should let both men know. The woman should not tell either man who the other one is to avoid confusion and problems. When a woman lets the new man know that she's leaving an abusive relationship, he should understand and be aware of the consequences of her departure. The woman should inform both men that she is trying to avoid domestic squabbles that may cause death, jail, or injury. When the woman is trying to get another man to help her get out of a bad relationship, she should reconsider involving him in her domestic mess.

## SHE DOESN'T WANT HIM, BUT SHE NEEDS HIM

A woman may not really want the new man, but she needs him to help her, so she uses him to the best of her ability. If the new man is a big man she uses him because she feels he can protect her. His size helps her antagonize the man she is trying to leave. Once her relationship ends with the ex she leaves the new guy to date someone else—someone she really wanted to be with in the first place.

## DON'T BEAT YOURSELF UP

When a woman breaks up with a man she shouldn't beat herself up about it. There's someone for everyone and maybe he just wasn't for her. She should not run around and tell everyone because many times men aren't responsible for what they do. To see what kind of man she's dealing with she should start a little harmless trouble up front when she meets him, to observe how he handles it. This way she'll find out whether he's weak, strong, passive, or whatever. Because women say, "I want a man with a little roughness around the edges," they think a strong man won't lose his composure and try to break down her door. A woman thinks he's going to straighten things out in a sensible way. She should know that if he doesn't straighten it out in the beginning he might end up acting a fool in the end.

## IT'S OKAY TO APOLOGIZE TO THE MAN SOMETIMES

There have been women who have gotten rid of good men because they were foolish. It's okay to apologize to a man and see what he's doing with his life now. Good men don't stay out there long because a woman will see the quality in him and grab him, even if she's a hoochie mama. Every woman wants a good man. Most women recognize a good man, but some of them start tripping because he's not as fine as she wants him to be. A woman should first see how fine the man's heart is and how clean his insides are before she starts looking at his alligator shoes and his suits.

If a woman would observe some of the silly things she's done, she'll see what kind of man she has. If she can see what kind of men she attracts in comparison to what kind of man she has, she'll learn a lot about herself. She should ask herself, "Why am I choosing this kind of man?"

## WHEN IT'S TIME FOR THE WOMAN TO LEAVE

Women like to ask men questions about men, but when the man gives a woman a truthful answer she responds as if she didn't hear him. When a man tells a woman that it's time to leave she doesn't want to hear it. She knows it's time, but she's afraid due to issues and circumstances or she simply doesn't want to start over. She feels bad about the decision to leave because she:

feels like she abandoned her family.
cannot afford to leave at that moment.
doesn't have a place to go.
doesn't want to disrupt her children's lives.

If you're in an unhealthy relationship and you ask your kids, they'll probably say, "Let's get out of here."

## IF YOU'RE GOING TO LEAVE, PLAN IT

A woman should not plan to leave until she writes it down on paper. Then she needs to analyze it. Don't just run out the door. That's a bad move.

## IF HE WANTS TO LEAVE, LET HIM GO

If he's trying to break away and she's holding his legs as he leaves out the door, he might come back, but he'll only come back to have sex with her. After sex he's right back out the door because he knows that he has time to play and mess around. She should say, "Okay, I trust your judgment, and I think it's a very wise thing for you to leave." As he leaves, she should tell him, "Have a good life." If he comes back begging and would rather listen to what she has to say, he might be ready to turn his life around and settle down. But the woman should not interrupt his begging and crying, because if she does she is setting herself back.

## LEAVING: A WOMAN SHOULD BE THANKFUL

When a man says, "You can leave if you want to," and suggests that the woman won't ever find another man like him, she should say, "Who in the world wants to find another man like you?" What a woman doesn't need is a person like the one she just left. A woman should ask herself why she left him in the first place. Why does she want someone like him? If she's going to find someone just like him, she might as well stay. She should simply keep the man she has if she's going to go out and find someone just like him.

## IS IT REALLY OVER

A woman has seen a man do it a million times. It's no different if he's a millionaire, or plays sports, or whatever. She's seen guys sit and tell the whole world that this will be the last game they ever play, and a year or two later they're right back playing ball. They came back for the game.

She's seen boxers fight their last fight, and then two years later they're in the ring, boxing again trying to make more money. She's seen singers say this is their last CD, only to come back and make another one. Everyone likes to make a comeback, but a woman should let the man go to do what he wants to do. Even though many women think men are robots, men do have hearts. Their feelings are tucked away where the woman can't reach them, but there's a woman out there who can get to his heart, no matter who he is.

## DON'T BE DESPERATE; LET HIM GO

A woman should quit thinking she's the only one who's in love and hurting. Men hurt too, but they don't put their hurt on display just because the woman is acting a fool with her pain. Once he sees her acting crazy and hollering and screaming about killing herself over him, he does what he wants to do anyway. By now the man knows she'll take him back any way she can get him. She's showing her desperation by acting a fool.

## LEAVING ONE RELATIONSHIP FOR ANOTHER

It's very difficult for a man to leave one relationship with a woman and get into another deep one immediately. This kind of man usually wants to hurry and get back in the dating game and find a new woman, but this is not always the rule. I decided while I was out of the game that it would be easier for me to go into a relationship that was sure to work. A woman should not set herself up for failure by waiting on a man. She should never sit and wait on him to get rid of a woman who he's not really thinking about getting rid of. And if he does get rid of her, he probably doesn't want the woman who's waiting on him.

## He's Gone, but It's Not Goodbye

Just because he said goodbye doesn't mean he's gone. The man is at her house and she hugs and kisses him goodbye. She even waves when he drives off, just to find out ten minutes later he's back knocking. He forgot something that belongs to him. That's the same way with a relationship. Just because he's gone doesn't mean its goodbye. The man can say, "I'm out of here," pack all his stuff, get down the street, and realize he left something . . . something that he really wants.

When a man says he's leaving the woman should let him go because it will be better in the long run. Don't beg him to stay. Just let him go and if he comes back, you might be able to keep him—if he's straightened up. If you feel touched by something and want to get the old feelings out of your body, write his initials on a piece of paper. Now tear it up and put it in the trash. If you really want him out of your life this will help you visualize ending the relationship.

## Moving On

One of the ways a woman can tell she's really getting over a man is when something that was hard to stop becomes easier. When she finds that she gets angry with herself for stupid things that she has done, she's almost over him. Even though she might do it again, she's so angry with herself for doing it that she'll say, "I can't believe

I did that again." She's on her way to recovery once she realizes that it wasn't the man who tricked her, but she tricked herself because of love.

The man often ends up leaving the woman just because she made threats to leave.

# Thirty

# ESTEEM

*Gather some strength from somewhere and get your life in order.*

A woman has got to quit blaming others as well as herself for what's going wrong in her life. The best thing for her to do is start looking at her life in the way God wants her to see it. God wants each of us to do something for Him and this book is my way of doing something for Him.

## HELPING OTHERS FEEL BETTER MAKES YOU FEEL BETTER

When a woman is at her lowest and she can't get up anymore, all she has to do is look at someone who's doing worse than she is. If she can do something to make that person feel better, she'll start feeling better. When a woman helps somebody less fortunate than she is, it makes her realize how good she really has it. She can feel good about helping them when they can't help themselves. She can mentor, fix a cup of coffee, sit and talk to them, fluff their pillow, whatever. Do something kind and watch how you begin to realize how good your life really is. A woman can also visit a bad area that's full of crime, condemned homes, and abandoned buildings, or go to a homeless shelter or anywhere people are doing badly and she'll understand better why she should quit crying about her life and do something about it. She can see why other people are having a hard time moving around.

## STOP THINKING THAT LESS IS BEST
I did a lot of no-good things, but I always had a good heart. I never tried to do anything else because what I was doing was working for me. I didn't feel at the time that I was all that bad because women kept accepting me as I was. If I messed up they would accept me back into that revolving door. The lesson here is that women should stop thinking less is best.

## DON'T LET PEOPLE MAKE YOU THINK YOU'RE CRAZY
Quit letting people make you think you are crazy. Quit letting people tell you that you are nothing and will never be anything. A woman should tell herself she's something and she's not crazy.

She should start believing in herself instead of letting other people tell her what she is. She should be what God wants her to be. When she hears people say, "Hey girl, you've been having it rough," or, "Lord, I don't know what's wrong, she's never going to come out of this," she should remember that she will come out of it because God lets us go through many things in our lives and in the end the blessings come. When that time arrives she should learn how to release all the other stuff and get it off her back. She should just walk free.

## A WOMAN NEEDS A PURE HEART
Somebody should come up with a liquid that women can drink that takes the hardness off their hearts and returns them pure—the way

God made them when women came into the world. It would give grown women a chance to see what it feels like to love somebody with a pure heart like a child would do. Sometimes a woman's heart has to be pure in order for her to accept the goodness a man can give.

## Do It for Yourself
A woman lets other people tell her who she is, what she's going to be, and how her life is going to be. If she can tell herself what she wants to be and how her life is going to be, she can do it for herself. Quit letting people do it for you and do it for yourself.

## To All My Big Girls
If a big woman has lost weight she needs to quit thinking "fat." She has to change the outside and the inside. She might have lost a hundred pounds, but she's still thinking fat. She's got to get rid of the fat mentality and start thinking bold and beautiful, curvy, voluptuous. If she doesn't get the fat thoughts out of her mind she'll go back to being fat.

## Be the Prize
In every box of Cracker Jacks there's a prize. There's plenty of popcorn, peanuts, and caramel, but there's only one prize, and if a woman is going to be something special, she has to make sure she's the prize. Why should a woman be popcorn or peanuts when she can be the prize?

## Men Work from a Different Perspective
A lot of times women need credit for things they have to do. The man ought to feel good about saying, "Baby, you look good today. Baby, you're doing a nice job." Men work from a different perspec-

tive. They say something only if something is wrong. As long as nothing is wrong or going wrong they appreciate everything they're doing through silence. That's just the way men are. They learn how to appreciate what a woman does through limited voice. Just because men don't tell women how they feel doesn't mean they don't feel or they don't see her.

Why should a woman be popcorn or peanuts when she can be the prize?

# Thirty-One

# LYING

*What I had to do is go past what a woman let me do and do what God wanted me to do.*

M ost lovers will lie when the truth will do. The main two killers in the world are heart disease and strokes. Even though many women know this they will still allow a man to worry them. They get so full of stress and hate that they can't think straight. A woman should simply change the way she feels about the man who doesn't feel anything for her because he might take her heart in another resting period. If she keeps letting men break her heart, it's going to get diseased, it's going to get weak, and it's going to fail. And that's the only thing that really keeps her alive, because when it quits beating so will she.

## BE UP-FRONT AND HONEST WITH HIM

If there's something wrong with you, like a disease, AIDS, herpes, or if you have a wooden leg, please put it up-front and tell the man. Why would a woman marry a man, then string him along? He'll end up leaving her in the long run. She doesn't have to tell a guy during her first date, but if the relationship is going somewhere, she should open up the lines of communication and just let it out. Tell him what the problem is. If he cares enough about her, then it really isn't a problem. If she's reading this book and knows that she's not a woman and trying to play like she's one, I think she'd better tell him that too. She shouldn't just sit there and tease him sexually and then when it's time for him to do it back she has a surprise for him. She tells him she's a man. In my world that's an instant beat-down. I'm talking about as soon as it's revealed to me. If I've already kissed him, that's a straight beat-down from me. That's probably a reason for murder, but I don't know right now, I'll just say a beat-down because I don't think anyone can ever get me in that position. I know what a woman looks like and I know certain things about a woman that I can look for that a man cannot fool me on.

## SOME WOMEN TELL ONLY HALF THE TRUTH

Women call me for advice and then they lie to me. They tell me half the truth. So when I get half the truth I can only give half the help. A woman like that is only fooling herself. She's not fooling me. If she tells me the truth about what really happened I could tell her what to do. If she's only going to give me half the truth this means she really doesn't want to know the truth. She thinks I'm going to tell her to leave him alone, so she hides part of the truth. You're not fooling me; you're really fooling yourself. Giving me the opportunity to tell you what I really think will make a difference in your relationship.

A woman should give her man a fair shot at making the relationship work.

# Thirty-Two

# GET A LIFE

*When the relationship is dead, a woman should have enough pride to move on and not beg a man to take her back. It's over!*

*Ladies, you're going to have to gather some strength from somewhere and get your life in order. You're got to be strong!*

A woman should get into life before life gets out of her. Her man has run off, she's gotten a divorce, and now she's bitter while she's raising the kids. She's raising her daughters to think that *all* men aren't good *to* women or good *for* women. Then the woman turns around and raises her sons to be nothing as men. A woman should be careful of what comes out of her mouth when she's raising her children because she's planting those same thoughts in their heads.

A lot of girls want to be like their mothers, but their mothers are male bashers. They hate men and their daughters are growing up automatically thinking that men are nothing because mama taught them to think and feel this way. If a woman has a son, she's mad because he looks like his daddy. She needs to change the way she speaks about her son's daddy. Sometimes her son will say, "Mama doesn't like me." He thinks mama doesn't like him because she doesn't like Daddy. He feels that if he looks like Daddy he's a reminder of Daddy to her—whom she hates. She has to realize when she is treating him different. He often hears his mom say that men aren't anything and that's planted in his head too.

## FREE YOUR MIND, TAKE BACK YOUR LIFE

If a woman stops letting her life take her where it wants to go and starts letting her mind take her life where *she* wants it to go, she'll be a better person for it.

## GO ON WITH YOUR LIFE

When the relationship is dead, *it is dead*! Why go back and try to relive it? A woman will spend years inside her soul trying to rekindle the relationship with a man, thinking, "I wish I had him back," knowing that it's over and there's no way he will take her back. She should let it die and move on. She should never spend so much time on the dead that she forgets the living and how to live. She should try her best to go on with her life. It's the living man who will be better for her than the man who has died in her life.

Get into life before life gets out of you.

# Thirty-Three

# DEATH

*Stand behind God and let God do the talking.*

She says that she's going to die when it's her time to die and that it's never too late to live. Well, sometimes it is too soon to die and too late to live. She's seen it. There are little humps in the ground and all of them aren't big headstones; some of them are kids. There are little bodies in those graves too. They say only the good die young. Well, I've had a couple of partners who were good and they died. I thought they were good, and evidently something happened where they were called home. God calls good people home at any time. Understand that if a woman is going to go away, she's got to go in a way that's meant for her to go, and cut all that foolishness out because her girlfriend said she should do it.

If it's not working, let God give you renewed strength to live a new life because dying ain't much of a living.

# A FINAL WORD ABOUT BOOM

BIG BOOM . . .
- Celebrated relationship speaker
- Entrepreneur
- Soon to be bestselling author
- Radio and television celebrity bodyguard

## A HIGH-ENERGY MESSAGE

Boom is a celebrated speaker, author, and celebrity bodyguard. He's the kind of man who will give you the shirt off his back in time of need, or tear the one off your back if you're the problem. Boom runs to trouble instead of away from it it. Boom has risen from his pimp days of hurting women to now protecting women as the bodyguard of women's hearts. His down-to-earth and warm colorful message tells women how to ducka sucka and protect their hearts while living up to the deserved greatness of good love. Boom the bodyguard of women's hearts gives up his playa card and reveals the secrets men have kept from women so he can help women obtain the fulfillment of their hearts' desires. Born into a low-income family in Tulsa, Oklahoma, Boom was not the priority in his family and craved constant attention. He became a bully to get attention and soon realized that women could easily become his victims. His mother was a single woman who had very little time or financial means, but had a very big heart. As a child, Boom's lack of attention to schoolwork, his lack of energy for doing the right thing, and the failure of his teachers to recognize his true potential resulted in him being mislabeled as a slow learner, which caused him to fear academics and suffer low grades throughout his schooling. This contributed to an unhealthy self-image and poor outlook on his life and the people around him. Boom is the American dream, overcoming adversity himself. It was a combination of his will to rise above his troubled background and a willingness to create a positive image for himself.

## PASSION TO FIND HIS WAY AND THE HUNGER TO REALIZE TRUE HAPPINESS

Boom has had no formal education, but with persistence and determination he has initiated and continued his process of self-education. It has distinguished him as an authority on harnessing human potential and matters of the heart. He turned to pimping and bullying his peers to gain a sense of power and self.

In 2005, Boom entered the public speaking arena as a bodyguard of women's hearts. The company provides books authored by Boom, relationship tapes and materials, and workshops aimed at individuals, groups, and organizations.

## THE BODYGUARD FOR WOMEN'S HEARTS

As a professional bodyguard Boom has provided for his celebrity clients conspicuous or inconspicuous protection services depending on the threat or potential hazards to the client. His capability to protect his clients lies in his ability to immediately assess and evaluate a threat or conflict and avoid a confrontation or defuse it before it escalates. He is now implementing his skills to protect women's hearts. With hard work and determination and after several failed marriages, he reached out to God. Boom has gotten on God's path to truly experiencing life and now speaks to women about how to avoid certain pitfalls and create, experience, and expect certain goals for their relationships.

## SOON TO BE BESTSELLING AUTHOR AND CELEBRITY

Boom has set out to be an internationally recognized speaker and author. He is in the process of negotiating to become the host of *The Boomerang Show,* a nightly television call-in show that focuses on relationship and love solutions rather than problems. Boom is a self-proclaimed leading authority on understanding and stimulating human potential in the area of love and relationships. He utilizes powerful delivery and newly emerging insights. Boom's customized presentation teaches, inspires, and channels audiences to new achievements.

"I used to say, "The more she cries the less she has to pee out." Now I say, "The more she cries the more her heart dies." — BOOM

# APPENDIX

## QUESTIONS WOMEN SHOULD ASK MEN

Here are questions women should ask if they are involved or thinking about becoming involved with a man. This questionnaire is anonymous, so you don't have to sign it. Answer only the questions that you are interested in. You don't even have to complete it. Just reply as you wish. You may choose not to answer any of the questions. That's okay too. You may want to create your own. Just send it in. Please mail questions, answers, and comments to:

Big Boom
5960 W. Parker Road
Suite 278-129
Plano, TX 75093

1. What has he been doing professionally for the last ten years?
2. Is he still staying with his mother?
3. Does he have children?
4. Has he ever been married?
5. What does he do?

6. What does he want to do?
7. Did he finish school?
8. Where does he work?
9. Is he married?
10. Does he have children or baby mama drama?
11. Is he currently dating anyone?
12. Is he gay or into that lifestyle?
13. What are his short- and long-term goals?
14. Which sections, chapters, or issues of this book do you agree with? Disagree with?
15. Which part of this book is the most important to you? Least important? Most emotional?
16. Have your views about men changed since you read this book? In what way?
17. Do you have supportive male friends?
18. Do you think that most men are uninformed about what pleases a woman?
19. What are your best relationship experiences?
20. How long do your relationships normally last?
21. Do you usually initiate the sex or the sexual advances?
22. Do you enjoy touching your mate?
23. During general caressing, was it difficult to do the first time you did it? How did you feel about it?
24. Do you like this questionnaire?
25. What else would you like to talk about?
26. Why did you answer this questionnaire?
27. Are you in love?
28. Does love make you happy?
29. What makes you happiest in life?
30. What's the gender of the person you are closest to?
31. What is your biggest relationship problem?

32. What is your favorite way to spend time alone?

33. How do you feel about pornography?

34. Have you ever had an affair or sex with a married man?

35. How often do you have sex with your partner?

36. Would your relationship with your partner be in danger if sex decreased?

37. How often do you want or like to have sex?

38. Has sex with your lover changed for the better? The worse? Has it become boring or more pleasurable?

39. Do certain conflicts in your relationship tend to last for years or over long periods of time?

40. Have you found that the same problems keep cropping up even after you've talked about them or thought that they were worked out?

41. What do you like most about your man? Least?

42. What do you tend to need most from your man, if anything? Is there something you get from men that you can't get from women?

43. What effect does falling in love have on you? Do you think men take falling in love seriously?

44. Have you ever been financially dependent on a man? What problems, if any, did it create? How did you feel about it? Did it ruin your relationship?

45. Have you ever been deeply hurt by a lover? How? What happened to hurt you? How soon did you get over it?

46. What emotional mood swings do you go through in relationships?

47. Have you ever hated a man? Describe the man you hated the most. Why did you hate him? Did you remain angry for a long time? Did you tell your friends? How did they react?

48. Have you ever felt like you had to work to keep a man? Did you have a fear of him leaving you? Of losing his love?

49. Did you ever feel that he would grow tired of you? Love you less?

50. Do you usually break up the relationship?

51. Do you ever feel that your sexual needs are unhealthy? Kinky? Dependent?

52. Do you feel that your love is too blind or too desperate?

53. Do you feel that your need for affection is excessive or over-bearing?

54. Do you feel more secure when in love?

55. Do you think that love is a problem for most women?

56. Are you afraid that you will make him feel tied down if you express your love to him?

57. Do you turn to men or women when in trouble?

58. What was the most important relationship with a woman in your life?

59. Describe your closest female friend. What is or was your relationship like?

60. Is love between women different from love between men?

Is this relationship healthy? Is it emotional and sincere?

61. Have you ever fallen in love with a woman? Would you like to fall in love with a woman?

62. Who is the person you have loved most in your life?

63. Who made you feel the most alive? The most loved and cared for?

64. How do you define love? Is falling in love the thing that you work for in a relationship over a long period of time?

65.  Was there anything that you would like to say but didn't or couldn't say?

Please add anything you would like to say that was not mentioned in this questionnaire at the end of it. This questionnaire is presented to make you slow down and pay attention to your relationship and possibly discover what shape it is in.

THANK YOU!
For information address:
Attn.: Big Boom
Bodyguard for Women's Hearts
5960 W. Parker Road
Suite 278–129
Plano, TX 75093

# AUTHOR PROFILE

Boom continues his self-education, which has distinguished him as an authority on harnessing human potential and matters of the heart. Boom's craze to learn and realize greatness helped him achieve a level of honesty about life. After several failed marriages he reached out to God and has since gotten on God's path to experiencing life and now speaks to women about how to avoid certain pitfalls and experience fulfilling relationships. Boom is a self-proclaimed leading authority on understanding and stimulating human potential in the area of love and relationships.